M000203623

Experiment!

Website conversion rate
OPTIMIZATION
with A/B and multivariate testing

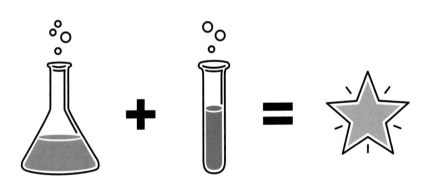

Colin McFarland

New
Riders

VOICES THAT MATTER™

Experiment!
Website conversion rate optimization
with A/B and multivariate testing
Colin McFarland

New Riders
1249 Eighth Street
Berkeley, CA 94710
510/524-2178

Find us on the Web at: www.newriders.com
To report errors, please send a note to errata@peachpit.com

New Riders is an imprint of Peachpit, a division of Pearson Education.

Copyright © 2013 by Colin McFarland

Project Editor: Michael J. Nolan
Development Editor: Rose Weisburd
Production Editor: David VanNess
Copyeditor: Gretchen Dykstra
Proofreader: Patricia Pane
Indexer: Rebecca Plunkett
Cover and Interior Design: Mimi Heft
Compositor: WolfsonDesign

Notice of Rights
All rights reserved. No part of this book may be reproduced or transmitted in any form by any means, electronic, mechanical, photocopying, recording, or otherwise, without the prior written permission of the publisher. For information on getting permission for reprints and excerpts, contact permissions@peachpit.com.

Notice of Liability
The information in this book is distributed on an "As Is" basis without warranty. While every precaution has been taken in the preparation of the book, neither the author nor Peachpit shall have any liability to any person or entity with respect to any loss or damage caused or alleged to be caused directly or indirectly by the instructions contained in this book or by the computer software and hardware products described in it.

Trademarks
Many of the designations used by manufacturers and sellers to distinguish their products are claimed as trademarks. Where those designations appear in this book, and Peachpit was aware of a trademark claim, the designations appear as requested by the owner of the trademark. All other product names and services identified throughout this book are used in editorial fashion only and for the benefit of such companies with no intention of infringement of the trademark. No such use, or the use of any trade name, is intended to convey endorsement or other affiliation with this book.

ISBN 13: 978-0-321-83460-7
ISBN 10:   0-321-83460-7

9 8 7 6 5 4 3 2 1

Printed and bound in the United States of America

For Elizabeth

Table of Contents

Part III: **Moving Forward** 107

Chapter 7: **On Analysis** 109

Chapter 8: **On Results** 121

Chapter 9: **Conclusion** 135

Chapter 10: **Recommended Reading** 141

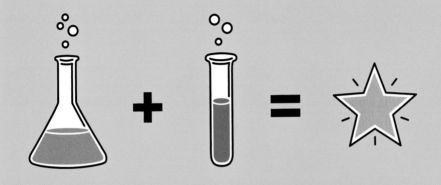

PART I

Getting Started

1

On Experimenting

Experiments

When you're involved in a commercial website, you're always seeking to improve it to yield more value for your business and for visitors. You could take a haphazard approach to improvement, try some stuff, guess what's working from looking at your metrics—the problem is noise in an uncontrolled environment is significant, and the metrics you're looking at probably aren't telling you anything. Or you could actually *know* which changes increase value, and by how much. Which would you rather do? If you prefer controlled measurement over guessing, great—you're an experimenter! Read on to learn what an experiment is, what it is not, and how to begin running one.

What an experiment is

An experiment is a means of gathering information to compare an idea against reality. To measure the impact of a new idea or existing experience, you observe website usage under conditions that are (ideally) identical except for the single aspect you're testing.

> An experiment is a means of gathering information to compare an idea against reality.

Your experiment could be on a small refinement, a new feature, a radical redesign from scratch, persuasive messaging, business logics, algorithm changes, pricing techniques, marketing approaches—you get the idea. As long as your hypothesis is clear, and you know what you're trying to achieve, you can test anything.

What an experiment is not

Eric Ries, author of *The Lean Startup,* captured it perfectly: "Experimentation does not mean shipping something to see what happens. If we do that, we're guaranteed to succeed—at seeing what happens. Something will always happen."

Experimentation requires a prediction, a hypothesis about what you expect to happen. You don't go in open-ended just to see what happens and look about until you're lost.

Where do I begin?

Let me say this up front: this book won't tell you exactly what you need to experiment, or offer you lists of low-hanging fruit, quick wins, or best practices. If you find them, let me know.

Instead, you'll learn what I think is much more useful: guiding principles that, in my experience, produce winning experiments. Consider this book the "how" to experiment, rather than the "what" to experiment.

First, let's look at where to begin, since beginning in the first place is the most important thing.

Start with the obvious

This book assumes you are reasonably adept at designing websites and are at least familiar with website usability (you're reading a book on experiments after all). Since you're implementing change on your website all the time, likely you already have ideas on what to experiment.

Those ideas you're already thinking about needn't get any more complicated. Start with the obvious! The list of obvious things to be experimenting includes:

▶ Calls to action (wording, size, color, prominence)

▶ Point of action assurances (free delivery, security)

▶ Badges (new, special, limited, sale)

▶ Headlines, copy, product descriptions (words, style, number of words)

▶ Forms (types of fields, length, layout, error handling)

▶ Layout and design (position and grouping of content, typography)

▶ Images and videos

▶ Shopping basket and checkout flow

If that doesn't do it, start by testing recent changes you made against their previous versions. You might be in for a few surprises.

There are no shortcuts

It's tempting to follow the lead of other experimenters in hopes of getting quick wins. But I encourage you to take their case studies, examples, and boasts lightly. You likely aren't seeing the whole story and have no way to know how rigorous the experiment was in the first place.

That's also the reason you won't find side-by-side variants from case studies in this book. Highlighting exact changes as spot-the-difference exercises focuses too much on implementation and distracts from the message and learning.

Instead of imitating others' methods uncritically, learn from their hypotheses and goals, and consider how you can apply the essence of their experiments to your own.

You need to do it yourself, get struck in, run a lot of experiments, and learn what works for you, your business, and your customers. It's time to get to work and find out for yourself how to win.

Takeaway

▲ Experimenting is making observations in regulated conditions.

▲ An experiment can be anything and can test any aspect of a site or service.

▲ Start with the obvious things so you can begin right away.

▲ There are no shortcuts and only one guideline: experiment!

Conversion techniques

Most likely, your aim when running experiments is to provide a lift in conversion—an increase from the control conversion rate to the challenger conversion rate.

> Your conversion rate is simply the percentage of visitors to your site who do what you want them to, such as making an order or booking a reservation of some kind.

Of course, some things make especially good experiment material for improving conversion. We'll look at these in this section, loosely grouped under Experience, Choices, and Behavior.

Keep these techniques front of mind as you start experimenting and learning the craft. With these as a focus, along with a strong hypothesis and a clear goal, you'll soon find winners.

Experience

Take things away

Chances are your site already has a lot of features and noise that don't add value, but in fact divert attention from the elements and features that do. This could be non-mandatory form fields, unnecessary promotional banners, features that aren't focused, or even just the aesthetic—anything that distracts.

Sometimes taking things away is just as good as adding new things. Before you add, experiment with taking things away to cancel the noise (see **Figure 1.1**).

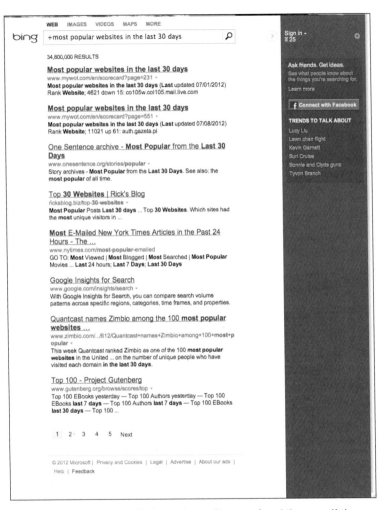

Figure 1.1 Based on a controlled experiment, Bing.com found there was little use of the search box at the bottom of search results and performance could be improved by taking it away.

Taking away gives you quick and easy experiment wins; but just as important, it prepares your site for the real work that follows. The less noise you have, the more your experiments can sing.

Customers have precious little time for your website. Don't be surprised when many of your early experiment wins happen simply by removing stuff you assumed was valuable.

Improve the user experience

Steve Krug said it best: don't make me think. A website that's easy to use and provides a great user experience (UX) is a website that converts well.

Experiment with simplifying and improving your website's UX, especially the tricky parts like registration forms, finding, sorting and filtering, product interactions, and purchasing funnels.

Some of your big wins will come through simply making it easier for customers to find what they want and complete the purchase. We'll talk more about UX in experiments in Chapter 3, "On Method."

Communicate clearly and design for delight

Talk to your customers like the emotional human beings they are. Experiment communicating more clearly through design (tell them where they are, where they can go, what's going on, and communicate using visual metaphors they understand) and language (use clear, active words and omit jargon and needless terms).

Understand that truly great user experiences delight customers. Consider the delight of using an iPhone; from the packaging to the user interface, every detail is considered. Try some experiments where you simply try to delight your audience. The attention is in the detail, and in experiments, detail is everything.

Choices

Most websites overload us with choices; choose from over 100,000 DVDs on Amazon, 24 million books on Amazon.com, and 15 million singles on Match.com. But as social scientist Sheena Iyengar demonstrates in her book *The Art of Choosing*, having too much too choose from can actually paralyze decision making and make us not choose at all: we think the profusion of possibilities must make it that much easier to find that perfect gift for a friend's birthday, only to find ourselves paralyzed in the face of row upon row of potential presents.

Paul Adams, in his book *Grouped,* also highlights a good example of how providing fewer choices can increase sales: when P&G reduced the varieties of its Head & Shoulders shampoo from 26 to 15, sales went up 10 percent.

Experiment with defaults, nudges (**Figure 1.2**), and badges to differentiate offerings and guide customers to make the choice that is right for them—or even any choice at all.

Guiding choices for visitors helps them commit to interacting with your website. By simplifying and guiding decisions, you'll prevent customers from giving up due to indecision.

Figure 1.2 As simple as it gets, Soocial.com improved conversion 28 percent with a gentle "It's free" nudge right next to the sign-up button.

Persuasion

In his book *Influence: Science and Practice,* Robert B. Cialdini identified six universal principles of persuasion: scarcity (the less available something is, the more we want it), social proof (we look to what others do to guide our behavior), liking (the more we like someone, the more we want to say yes to them), authority (we look to experts to show us the way), commitment/consistency (we want to act consistently with our commitments and values), and reciprocation (we feel obliged to return favors that have been done for us).

> Persuasive design is something that has been around for many many years, not least in the way high street stores and supermarkets lay out their stores to encourage and entice customers to buy as they arrive and walk around.
>
> In the online world, PET (persuasion, emotion, trust) is an approach that was pioneered by Human Factors International, and alongside usability and user experience, designing with persuasion in mind is an extremely powerful approach to positively impact on conversion rates.
>
> *"Booking.com: improving conversion with best practice persuasive design,"*
> *Paul Rourke, Econsultancy.com*

Every element of your website can be persuasive, and can play a role in moving your customer into the checkout funnel and completing a purchase (**Figure 1.3**). Optimizing the UX is the easy part; understanding persuasion in your website is uncovering what actually makes people buy. Make it your mission to:

▶ Understand what persuades.

▶ Consider persuasion design in every experiment you run.

▶ Make persuasion your number one priority.

Getting persuasion right is where you'll get huge returns on your investment in experimenting.

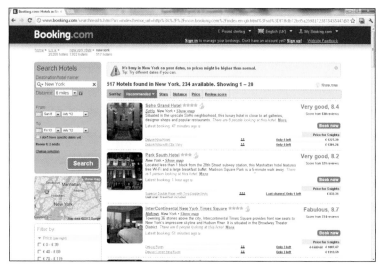

Figure 1.3 Booking.com put persuasion design through the heart of their website. Read Paul Rouke's fantastic breakdown on some of the techniques used to encourage customers to book a hotel at http://econsultancy.com/uk/blog/8151-booking-com-improving-conversion-with-best-practice-persuasive-design.

Dissuasion

It's all about removing reasons for visitors to leave the path they're on (**Figure 1.4**).

> Dissuasion is persuading someone not to take a particular course of action.

Dissuade customers from clicking Back, Home, or elsewhere. Focus them on staying on track to complete the desired action.

Experiment with giving customers the information they need at the point they need it, reinforcing through the journey what choices they have made and why they are right, and indicating progress and how little is left to complete.

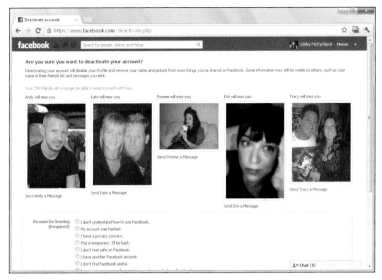

Figure 1.4 Facebook reduced account deactivations by 7 percent (a million more users a year) by making the deactivate account page much more emotional. Photos and names of the user's friends were added to the page, along with the statement "They will miss you" and a link to send them a message. This is a great example of using behavior and persuasion techniques in experiments.

Behavior

The field of behavioral economics also offers some techniques for increasing conversion. These relate to the mechanics of behavior, and can trigger compliance, an action, or an influence.

Behavioral techniques could be considered exploitative, especially when used for gain. I believe no design is neutral, so it's important to understand the behavioral impact of design changes. That way you can consider their implications in your designs and use your own judgment to decide what is suitable.

Here we look at two behavioral biases that are particularly prevalent in web design. Many more biases exist, should you wish to research further.

Anchoring

Anchoring choices to a point of reference is the mother of all behavioral biases; the result of using it is that people stay close to the point they were anchored to. It's used by virtually everyone who wants to sell anything, including supermarkets (multi-purchase offers make shoppers buy more than they would normally), car salesmen and real estate brokers (a high starting price anchors the negotiation), and, increasingly, web designers (defaulting an optional choice on a form increases the number of people who take it).

People tend to have an "anchor" price for most products, and judge them in relation to that anchor. For example, if you expect a laptop computer to be about $1,000, the $750 model might look like a bargain, but if you were anchored on $500, it'll seem expensive. Some products have very stable anchor prices (milk, bread), others change often (most electronics).

"Nissan's LEAF Creates a New 'Anchor' for Electric Car Pricing, Forcing Others to Match It," Michael Graham Richard, Treehugger.com

Framing

People's perceptions are easily influenced by the information that's presented to them. Creating frames is simply setting something in a different light that causes customers to look at it in a different way. Framing causes underlying behavioral bias to trigger in certain ways. For example, if you offer a magazine subscription that costs $2 a day, you'd likely get more subscribers if you framed it as costing less than a cup of coffee a day.

A study by psychologists Amos Tversky and Daniel Kahneman illustrates this effect (**Figure 1.5**).

Study participants were asked to choose between programs that could cure an impending disease. Participants were all given the same choices, but were exposed to different descriptions of the choices.

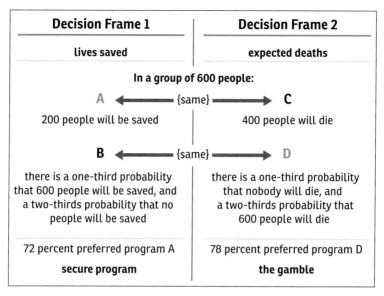

Decision Frame 1	Decision Frame 2
lives saved	expected deaths

In a group of 600 people:

A ◄——— {same} ———► C

200 people will be saved	400 people will die

B ◄——— {same} ———► D

there is a one-third probability that 600 people will be saved, and a two-thirds probability that no people will be saved	there is a one-third probability that nobody will die, and a two-thirds probability that 600 people will die
72 percent preferred program A	78 percent preferred program D
secure program	**the gamble**

Figure 1.5 Participants made different choices when the same data was framed in different ways.

Programs A and C would have identical results, as would programs B and D. However, the wording used to describe them had a marked effect on people's choices. When the choices were framed in terms of how many lives could be saved, people favored the secure program. When the same choices were framed in terms of how many deaths would result, people preferred to take a chance.

Takeaway

▲ Experiment with your website's user experience.

▲ Experiment with choices and persuasion.

▲ Understand that no design is neutral, and learn the behavioral impact of your experiments.

Create a plan for testing

You're probably beginning to get some experiment ideas by now, but don't rush into testing just yet. Before you run any experiments, it's essential to be clear on what you're trying to achieve. Let's look at creating a test plan that includes your experiment goal, hypothesis, and outcome.

Goal

Experimenting works best with one simple goal—an outcome that will be the definite answer to whether your experiment is good, bad, or makes no difference.

For most of us, reality is usually not that simple. Most businesses have more than one key performance indicator (KPI). You'll be concerned with primary goals like conversion and average order value (AOV), as well as secondary goals like registrations, quotes, and the like. For every experiment, you'll be concerned about the impact on all these KPIs.

It's important to set a simple goal for every experiment that indicates success, one that considers the importance of each KPI's impact on the bottom line. This means weighting your primary and secondary KPIs to give you a single view of an experiment's value. It's crucial to ensure this is a long-term goal that considers the lifetime value rather than simply short-term gains.

You could have different goals for different experiments. What's important is to apply the correct goal to each experiment. Since you've defined what success looks like up front, you'll know you're measuring every experiment fairly.

Goal examples

▶ **Simple goal (ideal):** Improve bookings. Increase demand. Increase registrations.

▶ **Complex goal (realistic):** Increase orders and AOV, OR increase AOV by 10 percent with no more than 1 percent loss in orders.

Now you're clear on what you want to achieve, let's move on to creating a hypothesis.

Hypothesis

Your hypothesis states what you think you'll find in your experiment. You're interested in finding a correlation between a specific variable (existing or proposed) and a specific outcome (positive or negative). When you build your hypothesis, you'll be making a plan to look for evidence that lets you say, "If we observe X, then it will prove that there must be a relationship between this variable and that outcome."

> **Hypothesis:** a tentative assumption made in order to draw out and test its logical or empirical consequences. (Merriam-Webster)

The hypothesis can support your experiment goal if you state it in terms of improving an OK thing, protecting a great thing, or finding a useless thing (so it can be replaced with a useful thing).

Improve

Your interest in running experiments likely stems from the desire to improve performance—sell more products, book more tables, get more subscribers, or increase something else.

Improving and optimizing is what experiments are made for. This will no doubt be the focus of your experiment efforts. As you reach experiment maturity, this will be your entire focus.

Protect

Improving performance is great, but just as important, and often overlooked, is protecting what you already have from loss through bad design choices.

Design choices fail all the time. The only way to ensure that changes don't have a negative impact is to experiment.

When you experiment and something fails, see what you have saved. If you didn't run an experiment, you wouldn't even know.

Make no difference

The idea here is to prove something has no commercial and measurable value, or makes no difference to your website, such that adding it or removing it would have no measurable impact on your bottom line.

If something makes no difference in terms of the hypothesis by which you're examining it, then you can question whether or not it has any value at all. This sort of experiment is especially useful for challenging the value of something that costs time, effort, or money to have on your site.

Experimenting to remove ineffectual things will free up real estate for future ideas, focus your efforts on areas that add value, and maybe even save you time and money.

The opportunity cost of poor hypotheses

Experimenting with something that won't produce a clear outcome or valuable learning for future experiments is an opportunity cost. Stay focused on finding winners that add real value to your business, and avoid pointless experiments.

> How much does it cost to go to a movie?
>
> Okay, now what's your answer if I told you that while the movie is taking place, you have to miss the final debate in the school board election, in a race where you're tied for first?
>
> Clearly, the stuff you miss has a cost.
>
> *"Opportunity Costs," Seth Godin, sethgodin.typepad.com*

Your hypothesis statement should literally include the words *improve, protect,* or *make no difference* to force you to focus, avoid vanity tests, reject personal preferences, and push back on stakeholder ideas that have no clear hypothesis.

Remember, just because you can test every idea, doesn't mean you should. There are better experiments you could be running.

Outcome

When planning your experiment, plan for an outcome. Always have a clear view of what's required to implement the winner and know how to make it happen when you're ready.

This will focus your efforts on change you can affect and avoid the frustration of producing results only to realize later that, for some unknown reason (legal, business, or other), the winner can't be implemented.

Takeaway

- ▲ In all experiments, create clear criteria to determine success.

- ▲ Experiment to improve, protect, or learn what makes no difference.

- ▲ Focus experiment efforts on changes you can ship.

Experiments fail

Failure, or the perception of it, is a huge part of experiments. Let's look at why you should accept failure, and understand that if your challengers aren't failing, you're not trying hard enough.

Accept failure

No matter how much you think it's a no-brainer, how much research you've done, or how many competitors are doing it, sometimes, more often than you might think, experiment ideas simply fail.

Failing to make your website better in an experiment is a powerful moment; it gives you the opportunity to learn about your approach and your customers (**Figure 1.6**). If you think a feature or change makes your website better, but your customers disagree (evidenced by how they behave, not what they tell you), then something about your approach and understanding of your customers can be improved.

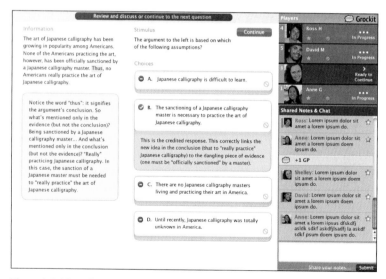

Figure 1.6 When Grockit.com switched to routinely running experiments on new features, they made a discovery: most of their new features did not change customer behavior at all! Now they accept failure in experiments as part of their development process and a crucial learning method.

When your challengers fail, accept it as a positive because you have learnt something. You know, through customers' actual behavior on your website in a controlled experiment, the direction you need to take.

Don't always expect to win

Considering the iterative nature of experiments and discovery, the idea of winning the first time and every time in experimenting is a ridiculous one. Yet that's how many businesses measure success, rewarding their experimenters on the amount of winners they deliver.

There's actually a risk here: focusing on the number of wins, rather than the size of the prize or the amount you're learning, encourages you to play it safe rather than challenge new ideas, and experiment only what you already know.

I encourage a different thought. Don't expect to always win the first time. (You won't.) Instead, realize the iterative nature of experiments: learn from your first test (usually called a wave) to adapt your future tests (the next waves), and so on.

Some of your biggest wins will come from many iterative experiments. But you'll also learn from some big failures.

> Our intuition is poor: [Most] ideas do not improve the metric(s) they were designed to improve.
>
> Based on experiments at Microsoft; ⅓ of ideas were positive, ⅓ of ideas were flat, ⅓ of ideas were negative.
>
> Google ran approximately 12,000 experiments in 2009, with only about 10% of these leading to business changes.
>
> *Ronny Kohavi, exp-platform.com*

Know when to move on

Now that you've come to consider experiments as an iterative process of learning and adaption, just when should you give up and move on to a new idea? Of course, there's no simple answer to this question. But as a guide, if you don't see positive changes in performance within five waves, park that idea for now and move on to something new.

As you move through these waves you'll become bolder and more focused in your adaptions of the experiment, naturally concentrating on learning the most you can from five attempts.

The nature of experiments usually means there are more ideas than capacity to test, so keep in mind that while learning is a crucial element, at the end of the day it's all about discovering and implementing winners that drive incremental profits.

Fail conclusively

As the famous Thomas Edison quote goes, "I have not failed. I've just found 10,000 ways that won't work." A properly designed experiment cannot fail, because even if your challenger doesn't win, you have learnt something: the control is better than this idea.

When your challengers do fail, it's important to let them fail conclusively. Otherwise, what you observe could just be random noise, and the challenger could actually have made no difference.

The worst thing you can do is stop an experiment before you know for certain that the challenger performs worse than the control. The learning you take from the experiment, if wrong, could have disastrous effects on your future approach to experimenting.

But fear not! To help you make this difficult decision, there's something called confidence levels. We'll learn more about them in Chapter 7, "On Analysis."

Takeaway

▲ Be brave enough to fail in experiments and accept the failure of challengers as lessons.

▲ Don't expect to always win the first time, but know when to give up.

▲ Fail conclusively to ensure that you don't take inaccurate learning from your experiments.

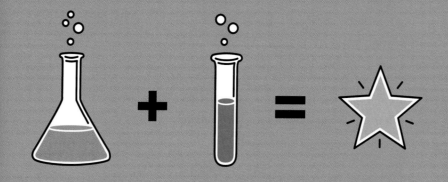

2

On Approach

Experiment today for the majority

Often experiment efforts fail simply because the time spent talking, planning, and meeting about what's going to happen makes it impossible to get an experiment out the door and learn from it in a reasonable time. Let's look at these challenges.

Experiment today

Shipping your experiments fast and often is crucial for success. The more experiments you get out the door, the more you learn and the more you win. Anything that slows you down is costing you.

> Always strive to improve the time it takes to get an experiment from idea to test. Look at the moving parts and throw away what slows you down.

When it comes to experimenting there's no time for perfection. Don't aim for the perfect experiment, aim for enough to get the experiment shipped—discover and improve from there.

Small projects

Start with what you can ship in two weeks. Aim for this to become what you can ship *every* two weeks. If it will take less time to implement the experiment and learn from it than it will to have a meeting about it, just ship it.

Consider anything that takes longer than two weeks a big project. Soon you'll naturally focus your development efforts on smaller pieces of work that can adapt. That's a good thing, because big projects often involve a painful process with time spent for no gain and further time required to learn what went wrong and how to fix it. It's better to ship early—fixing forward is a slippery slope.

Small experiments take only a short time to develop and ship, but that doesn't mean they're limited to small ideas. We'll talk more about small changes (refining the design) and drastically different changes later in the book.

Big projects

Don't neglect the bigger projects entirely. Big projects do have a place. Sometimes it's necessary to do more work to test an idea. Don't shy away from it, just find the balance so you can focus development time where it's needed.

Your results and experiment maturity at the time will lead you where you need to focus, but as a rule of thumb no more than one in ten experiments should be a big project.

Experiment for the majority

Focus your experiments on changes that affect many customers. This ensures that you're improving the big opportunities, not beating yourself up over edge cases. Experimenting for the majority also means more data coming in faster, which leads to quicker results and thus more wins.

Edge cases must die

Aim for completeness when designing and building experiments, but also realize that completeness isn't always possible while you're experimenting quickly in an agile way.

If getting something right for a small percentage of customers (for example, optimizing for Internet Explorer 6, or simply an unusual user journey) is delaying your experiment, exclude these edge cases (or accept the small impact), run your experiment, prove the value, then after you have a winner go back and do the housekeeping.

Breadth of exposure

While your goal and hypothesis should be sharply focused, make your experiment broad enough to capture the maximum potential opportunity in terms of traffic and visitors who will be exposed to it. Avoid specifics that cause you to miss many visitors and limit opportunity. For example, if your experiment applies to only a small product range or to a low-traffic area of a website, consider whether the same hypothesis could be applied to a bigger area.

> The more visitors who are exposed to your experiments, the more value your winners will deliver.

Target the majority

As you start learning from your experiments, you'll see opportunities to segment your visitors, such as new and repeat visitors, who would react differently to the same experiences.

Continue to target the major and valuable segments of your customer base. Make sure the cost of targeting outweighs any extra burden it puts on your experiment program.

Takeaway

▲ Focus on small projects (that doesn't mean small ideas), with an eye on the bigger pieces of work.

▲ Aim for improvement in your experiments, not perfection.

▲ Strive to shorten the time it takes to ship tests and move on to new experiments.

▲ Focus on experiments that affect many of your customers.

Control your experiments

When running experiments, control is critical. Let's look at some ways to feel confident that your experiments are controlled.

Why is control important?

Experimenting is a culture change from more traditional ways of designing websites; as such you'll meet a lot of resistance when you try to introduce a culture of experimenting. Communicating that your experiments are controlled will help reduce resistance and get people on board.

Control also ensures that you won't lose too much money while running experiments. You'll be able to notice bad experiments quickly and stop them. Additionally, control ensures that the results you're seeing are accurate and reliable.

Sometimes experiments lose money

Sometimes experiments cost money, make no mistake. Make that clear to your stakeholders up front. No matter how much you think you know about design, your customers, and your business, experiments have an associated cost and some of them will not result in the discovery of a valuable improvement. However, any loss is a controlled loss. You lose only for a short time until you realize the result is conclusive and stop the experiment.

> You could say experimenting is a bit like looking for gold. You won't find it the first time or every time, but when you do, the rewards will cover the losses many times over.

If your business can't afford to experiment, it shouldn't be experimenting. But you can't win if you're not prepared to lose. A loss is temporary; when you experiment and find winners, you'll gain the benefit forever.

How to control your experiments

Here are some things you need to get right to ensure that your experiments are controlled and to help you react quickly should they perform poorly and start costing too much money.

Eyes on performance

The ability to see how your experiments are performing at any time is the absolute minimum requirement before you get started with experimenting. Most vendor tools come preloaded with dashboards (see **Figure 2.1**), but dashboards are useless if you don't check them often. Always keep a close eye on how your experiments are doing—you can't just leave them in the background, you need to observe them all the time.

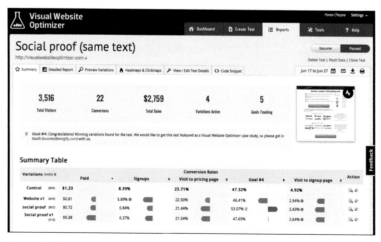

Figure 2.1 Keep your eyes on the performance of your experiments.

Kill switch

Being aware of performance is useful only if you can stop an experiment immediately should it go bad. Stopping an experiment can't wait for regular maintenance events such as normal site releases.

Make it as easy and fast as possible to stop a currently running experiment. Communicate to others how to do that in case of your absence. Most vendors make this easy. If they don't, wrap the vendor code that allows them to run experiments in a div tag with a unique name that's easy to find, so you can quickly remove the experiment by simply hiding the div or stripping it out of the code—call it a kill switch.

Mind the control

If you're running concurrent experiments, make sure that the variables of different experiments don't impact one another. For example, if you're testing white text on a black background in one experiment, and black on white in another at the same time, you'll get a combination where a site visitor gets white text on a white background. This would create a false negative and produce a misleading result.

> **Control:** A standard of comparison used to check the inferences deduced from an experiment. (Oxford English Dictionary)

Similarly, while running consecutive experiments, ensure that you're testing on a true control that has previous winners implemented. Let's say you found a winning challenger on the product page of your website and, while waiting for it to be implemented by your IT team, you found some other unrelated winning challenger on that same page. You can't be sure the second winner would have won in the presence of the first winner, since the first one itself is a significant change that should have been in place to create the correct environment for testing the second. Maintaining a true control through all experiments gives you much more confidence that you're driving profits.

Where possible, be aware of any external factors that could be introduced to your control and understand the impact (if observable) they could have on your experiment.

Takeaway

▲ Make it clear to stakeholders that experiments some-times lose money.

▲ Always have eyes on the performance of tests.

▲ Make sure it's easy to stop your experiments.

▲ Understand the implications of running concurrent and consecutive experiments.

▲ Pay attention to the control condition of your website.

Experiment everything

As you start out with experimenting, chances are you won't create an experiment culture overnight. Let's look at experiment maturity, so you can work toward an environment where you experiment everything.

Reaching experiment maturity

Ask yourself what would happen if the only changes you made were ones that were tested. Would your website be any better or worse? Of course, you won't know the answer, but I'd hazard a guess; your website would be more successful.

Experiment maturity is what every experimenter aims for: the point where you make all changes measurable through an experiment, where you focus on designing experiments, rather than just designing things that stakeholders or customers want.

Before you can reach maturity, you need to get started, you need to get wins, and you probably need to change the existing culture and ways of working at your business. Let's begin by looking at the stages of experiment maturity (**Figure 2.2**).

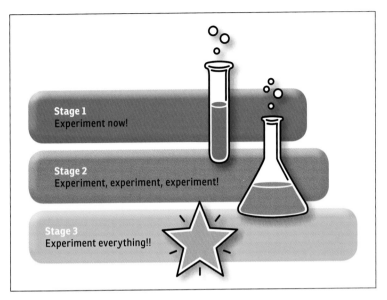

Figure 2.2 Experiment maturity model.

"Overstock.com has long considered ease of shopping one of the core components of great customer experience," said Seth Moore, Director of Customer Value at Overstock.com. "Rather than speculating about usability, however, we prefer to test the content and let our customers vote their preference with their actions."

In relatively little time, Overstock.com optimized its conversion rates and average order values by globally testing new product page layouts against current page layouts. To determine how various layouts performed, both at the page and category level, Overstock.com ran simultaneous multivariate tests to analyze a variety of scenarios on the site's shoppers. Similar tests were also run for promotional headers."

"Online businesses doing more with less in an uncertain economy via web optimization technology," Sitespect

Stage 1: Experiment now!

Get started and prove return on investment (ROI). The only way to start growing a culture of experimenting is to start doing it right now and get some results to talk about. Go for low-hanging fruit. Find a problem to fix. When your results show value, you'll put experimenting on the map, and get buy-in from your business.

> **ROI:** A performance measure used to evaluate the efficiency of an investment. To calculate ROI, the benefit (return) of an investment is divided by the cost of the investment; the result is expressed as a percentage or a ratio. ... The calculation for return on investment and, therefore the definition, can be modified to suit the situation— it all depends on what you include as returns and costs. When using this metric, make sure you understand what inputs are being used.
>
> (Investopedia)

These first experiments can even be failures. Saving the business money by preventing a change that would have introduced a negative is just as persuasive as a win.

It's even better if your result, positive or negative, is from a simple change that everyone in your business will understand. It will help them realize that all changes—even small ones they might never have considered—can have an impact on the bottom line.

Stage 2: Experiment, experiment, experiment!

Now that you've started, the goal is to grow your experiment depth, learnings, capacity, skills, and scope. Experiment often, prioritize your experiments, react to results in subsequent experiment waves, and move experiments across more business areas.

For some, this is a very short stage because the business buys into experimenting quickly and makes it a priority. For others, this might be as far as you can reach.

In this stage, your entire focus should be returning incremental value to your business and trying to reach the final stage, where everything is about experiments (**Figure 2.3**).

Figure 2.3 When you're using Bing.com today, you're typically in more than a dozen concurrent experiments.

Stage 3: Experiment everything!

At maturity, experimenting is your stakeholders' first thought. Most of what your business changes on the web is through controlled experiments. If you get here, you're in a good place.

There's no perfect experiment program. There will always be things you can improve, and more you can do. Even the best in this game, like eBay, Amazon, Google, Microsoft, Etsy (**Figure 2.4**), and Netflix, still sometimes can't experiment everything.

Don't stress about perfection. Aim to build a culture where you can continually improve, catch bad design choices, trial new ideas, challenge, and get the most out of your experiments.

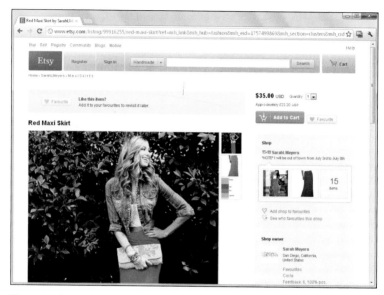

Figure 2.4 Etsy.com experiment as much as they can by baking A/B testing into the product release cycle so any new feature or design change becomes an experiment.

Takeaway

▲ Start by running simple experiments that prove ROI and get buy-in.

▲ Grow your experiment efforts and capacity, and aim to reach a culture where everything is about experiments.

Keep experimenting

Experimenting is a continuous process. If your hypothesis is correct, what's next? Be ready to react to wins (and failures) and push into the next wave of testing as soon as possible. Let's look at how to keep experimenting.

Maintain an open calendar

Having an open and flexible test calendar lets you base your next experiment on your previous ones. Pre-slotted experiment commitments over a long period of time allow no room to adapt and learn.

There's nothing worse than carrying out an experiment simply because you've committed to it, thus having to leave unexplored something you learnt from a recent experiment that has huge potential to drive value.

As you run an experiment, consider your options for the next experiment if this challenger is a winner, and also make plans for your next iteration if the current challenger fails. Although it's difficult to look beyond the juncture after the next, an ideal experiment roadmap shows the direction to move in depending on your current experiment's outcome.

Having your next turn planned out lets you focus on reacting to what you learn and saves you time, effort, and the opportunity cost of running poor experiments.

Think of these experiment rounds as waves, the first wave being what you are doing right now, the second wave what will follow, and so on.

Two-wave experiment roadmap (photocopy and keep)

▶ **Wave 1:** What's now (current test):

▶ **Wave 2:** What's next (if hypothesis is correct or incorrect):

Keep challenging winners

When you find experiment wins you'll naturally want to move on to experiment with something new, but don't neglect the winners. No one ever gets it perfect the first time.

Aim to make it better still. Maybe it's just squeezing that last drop of conversion out of it, or maybe it's a small tweak that turns a good experiment into a brilliant one.

The point is, you're not done. This is just the beginning. You should always think one wave ahead. When you're experimenting with wave 1, you should already be thinking of wave 2; when you move on to wave 2, you should be thinking of wave 3, and so on.

Don't rest on your laurels. Be ready to throw it away and start again. It's a huge problem when previous experiment wins become sacred cows and any new ideas are avoided because the old one was proven to work.

Reject that. Always be ready to challenge with something different. If it ain't broke, break it; you might find that something you thought was perfect wasn't so good after all. Or if your challenger doesn't prove better—great, you've just got more confidence that your previous win is as good as it can be. For now.

Revisit experiments later

While continuously experimenting and improving, sometimes you'll want to come back to an experiment for a second look. You'll certainly want to keep challenging winners, and occasionally give old contenders another chance.

Things change

On the web, change happens fast. New design standards rapidly catch on, customers' expectations quickly shift, and the online market you are competing in moves. Your website will now be constantly evolving as you experiment, make measurable differences, and roll out the winners.

An old experiment that may not have been quite right some time ago could now be ready since you've paved the way with other changes to your website that support it, give it focus, or make it more consistent.

From time to time, dust off one of those old experiments (naturally you'll want to keep records of your past work) that had something special but didn't win. Maybe now it's ready, or you learnt from other tests a new perspective that lets you tweak it to make it a winner. Remember, experimenting is a craft, and like any craft, sometimes making the best things requires patience and practice.

Repetition

Along the way, you'll want—and be challenged by others—to validate experiment wins by repeating them in another wave of testing. Repeating experiments is the hallmark of science. Being able to repeat an experiment with minor variations in the results lets you generalize the ideas and feel confident in relying on your learnings.

On the other hand, overfocusing on validation will get in the way of your experiment efforts and slow down progress. Find the right balance to enable you to make decisions and move on to the next idea.

Remember that you can always "undo" a winning experiment by reverse testing against the old control. Likely you'll quickly see the opposite result and demonstrate the value of your efforts.

Making experiments a way of life

Experimenting isn't something you can take or leave, something you can pick up when you feel like it. Forgive the cliché, but you really do need to live and breathe experiments.

Every day, think about what you can test, how you can do it better, what you're learning, and why the concepts you tested might have passed or failed. Think of every idea as a potentially great one that requires fair thought and attention.

Let nothing get in the way of improving your experiments program: your tools, your processes, your methods, or the people who work in or with your team.

Every experiment is just a new starting point. It will never be finished, it can always be better, and there's no such thing as perfect.

Takeaway

▲ Keep an open and flexible calendar for your experiments.

▲ Keep challenging winners, and improving further.

▲ Revisit previous experiments occasionally.

▲ Think of experiments as a way of life.

Bravery and responsibility

Experimenting requires the right mindset to achieve success. Let's look at two crucial elements: bravery and responsibility.

Bravery

When many businesses start experimenting, they begin with small, safe experiments to test the water. But these often do very little, and perhaps don't drive any actionable output.

Forget testing the water—you need to dive in. Find and experiment with the biggest issues on your site, and challenge the biggest assumptions of your business.

To get testing embedded in your culture, be brave, tackle the big things, and put experimenting on the map.

Responsibility

Let's get it straight: it's important to know who's responsible for experiments. A testing program without clear ownership is asking for big trouble in the form of untrustworthy data, muddy results, and eventual abandonment.

Who owns testing?

Everyone owns it, and that's the way it has to be to ensure success. All the moving parts of your business (brands, marketing, UX, development, IT, and so on) need to get behind the idea of experimenting and discovering, and become committed to helping it mature.

Engagement across your business will help you build a pool of ideas and expertise, and ensure that testing doesn't become a cottage industry serving only one aspect of the business or one person's ideas of what's important. You'll achieve far more useful results if you combine the strengths of your entire business.

But, you need a champion

Every experiment program needs a champion who's responsible for all experiments, a person who makes the call when to go, when to stop, when to ship, and when to quit. Every program needs someone to challenge the biggest assumptions, find the biggest opportunities, drive the priority, and get the best out of experiment efforts.

Without a champion, experimenting becomes a sort of organized chaos, with influences happening without control, well-devised hypotheses based on ill-devised approaches, and test plans with no focus on business goals. People won't have confidence in your experiments and you'll never build a culture of experimenting. In the worst-case scenario, you could end up with conflicting experiments that cause problems on your website for your customers.

If you don't have one already, get an experiments champion today. Make that person responsible and support them in the challenges ahead.

Be responsible for shipping

Optimization counts only when you ship winners. So many experiment programs fail because analysts see recommendations as the output and no one implements. Responsibility doesn't end at the end of your experiment. Don't create recommendations; instead, be responsible for shipping your experiment wins.

If you have the authority to make change happen, hold yourself accountable for changes so that when you find winners you'll ship them (**Figure 2.5**). If you don't, it can be a huge challenge. In Chapter 8, "On Results," we'll talk about how to present and communicate the value of your experiment results clearly so you can make change happen.

Figure 2.5 "Stay focused and keep shipping," from the desk of Mark Zuckerberg at Facebook.

Takeaway

▲ Experiments are for the brave; be brave and tackle the big things.

▲ Understand that everyone owns testing, but have a champion.

▲ Be responsible for shipping winners.

3

On Method

A/B and Multivariate Testing

We've talked about an approach to experimentation. In this chapter, we'll look at two methods you can use to actually run your experiments online: A/B testing and multivariate testing (MVT).

What are A/B and MVT?

A/B and MVT are methods for running controlled experiments online. Programmer Jesse Farmer describes it as a cage match: send in your champion against a challenger (or several challengers) and out comes a winner.

These methods let you compare alternative versions of the same page or element running simultaneously on your website by randomly assigning visitors to different groups, then comparing the data to see which version produces the best outcome for your goal, for example, increased conversion.

A/B testing

A/B, also called split testing, lets you experiment one against the other (**Figure 3.1**). You'll have a control page and a challenger page. You can also test more than one challenger against the control (A/B/n), but the results will show you only how each performs relative to the control.

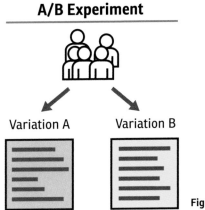

A/B Experiment

Variation A   Variation B

Figure 3.1 A/B testing.

Multivariate testing

MVT allows you to test multiple factors, each with multiple conditions. Let's say you sell sausages in Seattle. The things you might want to experiment with could be tagline, call to action, and image. **Figure 3.2** illustrates some possible combinations.

	Condition 1	Condition 2
Factor A Tagline	The World's Best Sausages	The Sausage Factory of Seattle
Factor B Call to action	**Buy 2 Sausages, Get 1 Free**	**Free delivery on all sausages Buy now**
Factor C Image on site		

Figure 3.2 Multivariate (MVT) testing.

Which method should I use?

The method you choose will depend somewhat on which stage of maturity you're at in your experiments program. (We discussed the experiment maturity model in Chapter 2, "On Approach.") Let's look at where the methods might apply.

Stage 1: Experiment now!

You're focused on testing fast and delivering results; A/B testing is the perfect method. Using a simple hypothesis, you can get fast results to prove ROI.

Stage 2: Experiment, experiment, experiment!

You'll continue to A/B test but introduce MVT to bring greater depth and learning where suitable.

Stage 3: Experiment everything!

You'll choose a method based on the complexity of the hypothesis you're going to experiment. You'll be using both methods simultaneously.

In a nutshell, your choice depends on whether you're constructing a simple test idea or a complex one. If your hypothesis is basic and you're testing only one factor, A/B testing is the natural fit. If your hypothesis involves testing two or more independent factors, MVT is better. MVT yields deeper insights, while A/B is speedier and simpler. Opt for the method that suits the task at hand.

The case for A/B

The benefits of MVT do come at the cost of simplicity and speed. If you want easy, fast, and focused experiments, look to A/B testing.

▶ A/B testing forces you to focus. MVT can tempt you to add unnecessary complexity to the experiment.

▶ A/B testing requires less traffic and takes less time to reach conclusive results.

▶ A/B testing is faster to develop and easier to submit to technical quality assurance than MVT.

Over the past decade, the power of A/B testing has become an open secret of high-stakes web development. It's now the standard (but seldom advertised) means through which Silicon Valley improves its online products.

"The A/B Test: Inside the Technology That's Changing the Rules of Business,"
Brian Christian, Wired

The case for MVT

There are obvious benefits to running an MVT test.

▶ MVT lets you experiment with many independent factors at the same time, hugely increasing the ability to learn and discover.

▶ MVT tells you not only what the winners are, but also the most and least influential variables in your experiment. An A/B test will only tell you the winner, and won't capture interaction effects.

Takeaway

▲ The stage you're at in your experiment maturity helps to determine the best testing method.

▲ A/B and MVT each have strengths and weaknesses.

▲ Choose the method that suits the task at hand: A/B for speed, MVT for depth.

Gathering the data

How long will it take? That's one of the most common questions when planning experiments. In this section, we'll look at how to answer that using the concept of minimum detectable lift.

When do experiments end?

You can never predict exactly how long you need to run an experiment to get results. It could be that there's no difference in the performance of your variants, so no matter how long you wait you'll never get a sample of data big enough to make you certain it's time to end your experiment.

> The experiment aiming to demonstrate that tar pitch is fluid has been running for more than 80 years. ... Professor Thomas Parnell... heated a pitch sample, poured it into a funnel, and waited for it to cool... for three years. Once it was settled, he broke the seal of the funnel's stem, and waited for the tar pitch to drip out. And it did! After eight years, that is.
>
> For quite some time, the experiment (protected by nothing but a bell jar) had been in danger of being thrown out if not for John Mainstone, who joined [the University of Queensland's] physics faculty back in 1961.
>
> If you're wondering how long it will actually take for the experiment to be marked complete, Mainstone says, "it has at least 100 years left if someone doesn't throw it out."
>
> *"Watch the world's longest-running experiment on webcam," Y!Tech*

However, you can use the lift you expect from your experiment (let's say you're aiming for 1 percent lift), along with your current website performance and the number of variations in the experiment, to show you the potential amount of time it could take to reach confident results.

Duration calculator

Visual Website Optimizer (VWO) provides a free, simple spreadsheet duration calculator (**Figure 3.3**). You enter the following four pieces of information and the calculator gives you the number of days you can expect to run the experiment:

▶ Conversion rate of original page

▶ Expected improvement in conversion rate

▶ Number of variants in the experiment

▶ Average number of daily visitors to the page

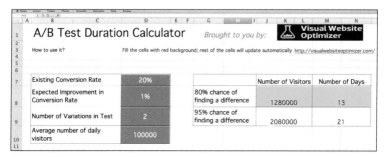

Figure 3.3 Experiment duration calculation using Visual Website Optimizer's free calculator at http://visualwebsiteoptimizer.com/split-testing-blog/ab-test-duration-calculator/.

Avoiding long durations

Another benefit of using this calculator is preventing experiments from taking too long to be worthwhile. If your duration is coming out as many months, you have three options to try to reduce it:

1. **Simplify the experiment.** The more variants you add, the longer it will take to reach confident results.

2. **Be bolder in your experiment design.** It will take less time if you expect to achieve a bigger lift in your experiment.

3. **Expand the experiment.** If you can expose the experiment to more traffic, it will take less time to reach confident results. For example, if it applies only to a low-traffic portion of your website, can you expand it to capture more visitors?

Ending experiments too soon

If you stop your experiment before it is complete, you could conclude with wrong results. You should stop before the recommended duration only if your experiment produces much bigger differences than you originally expected.

It's also good practice to run your experiments for at least two business cycles so you have confidence that your experiment performance persists over time. A business cycle is typically one week, allowing for work-day and weekend effect. We'll look at that more closely in Chapter 7, "On Analysis."

Takeaway

▲ An experiment will never reach its end if the variants don't drive a difference in performance.

▲ Use the duration calculator as a guide for how long to run your experiment.

▲ Avoid running an experiment that will take too long to reach confident results.

Traffic and exposure

Another frequent question while experimenting is how many visitors will see the variant you're testing. Your data will have to be derived from enough site visits to ensure that it's an accurate representation. In this section, we'll look at ramp-up traffic and exposure.

Ramp-up

Almost all major vendors (we'll describe them in more detail later in this chapter) offer you control over the amount of traffic you expose to your experiment.

You could choose, let's say, 10 percent of traffic to be exposed to the challenger. That means that 90 percent of the visitors to your website during the experiment duration will get the control condition and won't experience your challenger.

Experiment full-on

Always aim to experiment full-on, to make all visitors to your website part of the experiment. You'll spend less time running the experiment, you'll get data quicker, you'll move on to the next experiment sooner, and you'll learn more—and faster.

Use ramp-up sparingly, when you have no other choice. Don't let ramp-up become a wimpy way out. If you don't think an experiment is worth full-on, why are you even doing it?

Sometimes, though, there are reasons to begin with a gentle introduction.

Ramp-up can be useful

You can use ramp-up to get buy-in for sensitive experiments that are meeting some resistance. Experimenting on a smaller portion of customers will be perceived as less risky.

Start your experiment with a small traffic exposure, say 10 percent exposed to the experiment. After you've shown stakeholders that the world hasn't ended, you can ramp it up to full-on.

> Don't combine results from measurement periods that have different traffic exposures, or it will contaminate your data. Simply throw away the data from prior to the ramp-up.

Exposure

Less traffic exposed to an experiment doesn't actually mean less exposure; it just means you'll have to run the experiment for longer. The number of experiment participants required to reach statistical confidence will be the same, just spread over time.

Figure 3.4 illustrates this clearly. Experimenting full-on (100 percent of traffic), this experiment could expect to conclude in 21 days. Experimenting only to 10 percent pushes the experiment duration to 208 days.

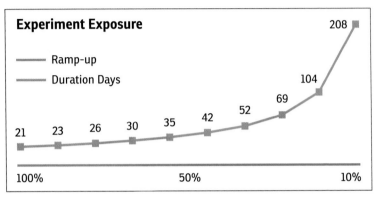

Experiment Exposure

208

Ramp-up
Duration Days

104

69

52

42

35

30

26

21   23

100%   50%   10%

Figure 3.4 Exposing less traffic to your experiments means you'll have to run your experiment longer.

Takeaway

▲ Always aim to experiment full-on so you get results more quickly and conclude more experiments overall.

▲ Use traffic ramp-up to get stakeholder buy-in for sensitive experiments.

▲ Measurements shouldn't be combined when one of the conditions under which they were made, such as traffic exposure, is different.

▲ Remember that ramp-up increases the experiment duration.

Unconventional methods

As you get smarter with your experiment efforts, you'll realize the power of the tools you have for measuring the value of anything. Let's look at some slightly less conventional methods for experimenting.

Fake it till you make it

At times you'll have experiment ideas that simply won't be feasible. Perhaps a change you want to make is too resource-intensive on your web servers, a new feature requires development that you're struggling to get prioritized, or your idea requires some software or system that you can't get funded.

You could accept that and move on to something else; I'm sure you won't be short of ideas. Or you can fake it. Use the flexibility of the tools at your disposal to recreate or rebuild (or build a small part of) the experience you're trying to achieve.

Hypothetical example

Problem	You want to experiment adding a Hot Item roundel to images on the gallery of items that have been selling quickly in the last few hours, but it requires IT development work to associate the products.
Fake it	Run an experiment with the Hot Item roundel attached to a random selection of product images.

When you prove the worth first, the desire to do it will follow. The resource constraint, development priority, or funding that held you back may take care of itself when you have a proven benefit to show.

The cost of taking it away

The value of some aspects of your website, like customer reviews, cross-selling activity, or a cool feature, might seem hard to quantify. But business relies on measuring and putting numbers on as many factors as possible.

You can help with a quick experiment. Show the cost of *not* having a feature by taking it away (**Figure 3.5**). Run an experiment where you simply remove it. You'll be a hero for helping to quantify what was thought to be unquantifiable.

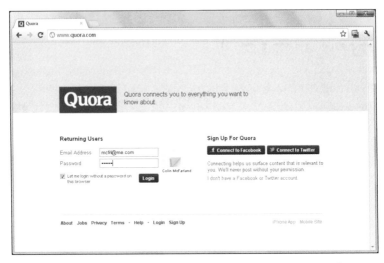

Figure 3.5 Quora.com, the popular question-and-answer site, has a cool feature on the login page. When you enter your e-mail address, the page looks up and displays your name and avatar before you enter your password. Pretty cool, but does it add any value? What if they ran an experiment on that?

Takeaway

▲ Fake things first through experiments to build a case for making it properly later.

▲ Learn the cost of not having something by taking it away in an experiment.

Tool comparison and install

If you've got this far in the book, you're ready to start experimenting. But before you can do that, you need the tools to support you. In this section, we'll look at some options.

Vendor tools

The technology required to run experiments is less complicated than you might think. Most vendors do a similar job, and all, regardless of price, will certainly get you experimenting right away and returning value on your investment.

One self-service tool you can get started with today is Google Website Optimizer (GWO). It's free and easy to install: you need only add some code to the head section of your website.

When you're ready to take on more complex experiments and increase the capacity of your efforts, look toward to the midrange tools like Visual Website Optimizer (**Figure 3.6**) or Optimizely.

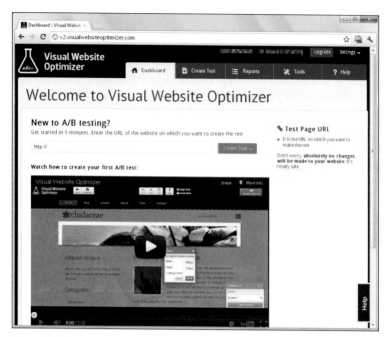

Figure 3.6 Visual Website Optimizer is an easy-to-use A/B and MVT tool that lets you create your first experiment in under 5 minutes.

Here's how easy it is to install Visual Website Optimizer. Simply create an account and get your tracking code, like this demo:

```
<!-- Start Visual Website Optimizer Code -->
<script type='text/javascript'>
var _vis_opt_account_id = 15459;
var _vis_opt_protocol = (('https:' == document.location.protocol) ?
'https://' : 'http://');
document.write('<s' + 'cript src="' + _vis_opt_protocol +
'dev.visualwebsiteoptimizer.com/deploy/js_visitor_settings.
php?v=1&a='+_vis_opt_account_id+'&url='
+encodeURIComponent(document.URL)+'&random='+Math.random()+'"
type="text/javascript">' + '<\/s' + 'cript>');
</script>
```

```
<script type='text/javascript'>
if(typeof(_vis_opt_settings_loaded) == "boolean") { document.
write('<s' + 'cript src="' + _vis_opt_protocol +
'd5phz18u4wuww.cloudfront.net/vis_opt.js" type="text/javascript">'
+ '<\/s' + 'cript>'); }
// if your site already has jQuery 1.4.2, replace vis_opt.js with
vis_opt_no_jquery.js above
</script>

<script type='text/javascript'>
if(typeof(_vis_opt_settings_loaded) == "boolean" && typeof(_vis_
opt_top_initialize) == "function") {
        _vis_opt_top_initialize(); vwo_$(document).ready(function()
{ _vis_opt_bottom_initialize(); });
}
</script>
<!-- End Visual Website Optimizer Code -->.
```

Then insert the code in your header on all pages of your site that you wish to track. If you have a template for the head, put it here and it will exist sitewide:

```
<html>
  <head>
    ... your website's head content ...
    Visual Website Optimizer code goes here
  </head>
  <body>
    ..... your website content ....
  </body>
</html>
```

When you've inserted the code, log in to your VWO Dashboard. There you can see whether the code has been inserted correctly and start building your first experiment. The tool is easy enough to use without instruction, but if you need some help, there are supporting documents on the site.

Taking it further still, heavyweights like Adobe Test & Target help you get smarter in terms of segmentation and targeting.

Check out the unbiased reviews on whichmvt.com, and find the tool that works best for your needs, budget, and the stage of your experiment maturity.

Developer tools

If you operate in a roll-your-own type of business, your developers may want to look at building their own platform that does exactly what you need and works seamlessly with other business systems.

Again, this isn't as hard as you might think. Plenty of supporting material exists online for developers building a custom platform. In fact, perhaps they don't need to start from scratch at all; there are prebuilt frameworks that they could build upon. One example is Vanity, shown in **Figure 3.7**.

Figure 3.7 Vanity (vanity.labnotes.org) is an experiment development framework for Rails.

The right tools can give you flexibility and features to run your experiments, but they won't make you the world's best experimenter. Ultimately, you'll still have to design and execute winning ideas, and you can do that with the simplest of tools.

Takeaway

▲ Choose the tool that matches your business needs, the stage of your experiment maturity, and the support and capacity you need.

▲ Remember that the tool is only the vehicle: it won't give you winners on its own. It's up to you to design and execute winning experiments.

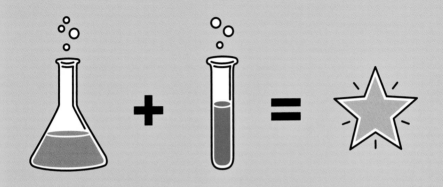

PART II

Interlude

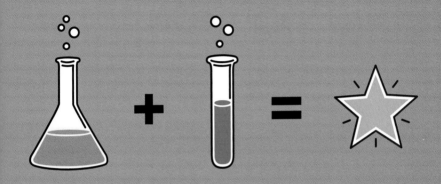

4

On UX

Design considerations

The most voiced concern for designers is that experiments encourage only small changes and thus stifle creativity. The thought is that experiments are suitable when you want to know which small detail, like button colour, is better, but you should go with your gut when you want to design a new masterpiece.

No doubt these ideas are encouraged by the case studies and examples you'll find on the internet. They show almost exclusively minimal changes that deliver big wins. There's little discussion of experimenting with major design projects. You can and should use experimentation for both refinements and drastic redesigns.

The big picture

Running a few experiments will give you a sense of which approaches are the most persuasive to visitors, and what areas of the site are the most influential. Naturally, you'll want to focus on these areas for maximum effect. Over time this will lead to incrementally smaller changes (**Figure 4.1**) that might cause you to drift away from the big picture.

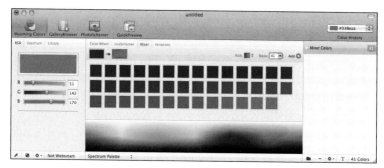

Figure 4.1 Marissa Mayer, former vice president of search products and user experience at Google, asked her team to test 41 shades of blue to see which got more clicks.

Incremental improvements

Google's Scott Huffman recognizes the danger that an experiment-centric business can become too focused on incremental changes and neglect the bigger breakthrough changes: "Testing tools can really motivate the engineering team, but they also can wind up giving them huge incentives to try only small changes. We do want those little improvements, but we also want the jumps outside the box."

Designer Douglas Bowman felt this frustration in his time at Google: "Yes, it's true that a team at Google couldn't decide between two blues, so they're testing 41 shades between each blue to see which one performs better. I had a recent debate over whether a border should be 3, 4, or 5 pixels wide, and was asked to prove my case."

Google is right of course to experiment every change—for them, a small drop in conversion would be a loss of millions of dollars. But if you find yourself experimenting something as miniscule as Douglas Bowman's 5-pixel border, maybe it's time to reconsider your approach, and aim for bigger wins.

Innovative leaps forward

Incremental design and innovation can go hand in hand. You can run an experiment on anything. You can test an incremental change, or you can test anything from an innovative new feature to an entire redesign. To get the most from your experiments you should be doing both: continually delivering incremental improvements, while never losing sight of the big picture, the big opportunities, and the breakthrough changes.

In Chapter 2, "On Approach," we discussed the need to ensure some experiment capacity for bigger projects, to allow the room for truly innovative ideas to grow. We'll talk some more about innovative ideas in Chapter 6, "On Ideas."

> [O]ne of the hottest debates in innovation [is about] the value of metrics. It throws into sharp relief two seemingly opposed ways of thinking. The first is that decisions about new ideas should be based on evidence. The second is that new ideas can't be measured in advance. These two views are born of bitter experience. The experience of traditional business managers is that it's easy to be fooled by intuition, while the experience of traditional designers is that measurement can kill imagination. Yet what seems like a paradox actually hides a more interesting truth—that measurement and imagination are locked in a dance.
>
> *Marty Neumeier*, The Designful Company

Holistic user experience

Picture Frankenstein's monster, with parts bolted on here, there, and everywhere. UX designers worry that using experiments as the basis for design decisions creates a "Frankensite," if you will, whose experience lacks a holistic interconnectedness.

This is a valid concern. As you introduce winners from many experiments, your site's user experience will no doubt become a little fragmented. If you're not mindful of cultivating a good user experience in your experiments, your website can eventually become a malformed monster.

Don't stitch together a monster

You can avoid introducing major inconsistencies by striving incrementally toward a big picture for your website. Of course, this picture needs to be repainted often to adapt to what you're learning and the direction you're taking based on new results.

This big picture will likely be something aspirational that reflects the position of your brand and the way your business wants to be seen or positioned in the market. The big picture should be more than a mission statement; it needs concepts and mock-ups so it can easily be conceptualised.

> As the creators of the user experience, UX and design teams are ultimately responsible for keeping the website focused on the big picture, but it's important to represent all stakeholders and hopefully have some buy-in. You might also find that the big picture helps reduce stakeholders' resistance to a specific experiment, since it's clear up front that each experiment is a small step in a long journey toward that bigger goal.

It's also a good idea, every so often, to run an experiment that simply brings together the parts of your website experience that have become fragmented. (Of course, be sure not to introduce any negatives in doing so.) So, if you see a Frankensite beginning to develop before your eyes, round up all the abnormal pieces and reshape them in one operation to bring them back into an integrated user experience.

Netflix tests across all devices, including desktop, mobile, and apps, and manages to maintain a consistent and simple user interface. Chief Product Officer Neil Hunt shares that Netflix tests almost everything, from calls to action to algorithmic changes in its recommendation engines, to performance components like page load time, streaming time, and quality. Hunt summarizes the company's learning in three words: "simple trumps complete." Keeping simplicity at the heart of experiments helps Netflix deliver a smooth and adaptable user experience across devices (**Figure 4.2**), so whether you view your movies or rental list on a desktop, an iPhone, or a PlayStation 3, it always feels like Netflix and one coherent journey.

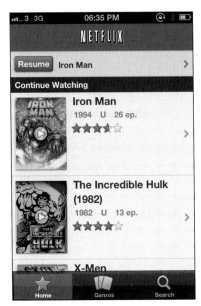

Figure 4.2 Netflix experiments almost everything across all devices, and still maintains a simple and consistent user experience (http://www.quora.com/What-types-of-things-does-Netflix-A-B-test-aside-from-member-sign-up).

Avoid consistency hobgoblins

While delivering a holistic user experience is important, don't let fear of inconsistencies hold back your experiments. You can always return to an inconsistency, but you can't return to something you haven't yet discovered because an idealistic view on user experience prevented you from running an experiment in the first place.

Give rise to generalizations

As you experiment with incremental improvements, small changes may give rise to generalizations. An experiment to determine whether a border should be 3, 4, or 5 pixels may be a tiny experiment in itself, but could lead to a fundamental insight that can be applied multiple times to many borders. You could create principles to capture these generalizations and use them to inform future design decisions.

Takeaway

▲ Keep the big picture in mind as you make both incremental changes and innovative leaps forward.

▲ Avoid fragmenting the user experience by incremental changes that drift from the design.

▲ Don't let consistency with the current user experience prevent you from experimenting to find even better solutions.

▲ Remember, sometimes studying something tiny can lead to fundamental insights.

Best practices

As we saw in Chapter 2, "On Approach," a good user experience is key to a high-conversion website. Usability or user experience best-practices guidelines are, of course, worth considering as you design interface elements to test against the current ones, but issues arise when best practices are considered no-brainers and implemented without any further thought.

It's easy to see why this happens. Best practices can become pretty convincing; after all, if everyone else is doing it, it must be good, right? If you've read this far, you'll know it's probably not that simple. The only way to understand if a best practice was the best design, or just a better design than you had before, is to break it and try something else (**Figure 4.3**).

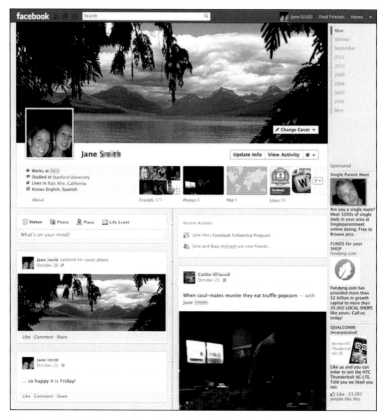

Figure 4.3 Nick Felton and Joey Flynn, who designed Facebook's Timeline, realized that when creating a page to tell someone's life story, they had to throw out the user interface rulebook and start something drastically different.

Make no assumptions. Challenge even the most obvious and convincing best-practices guidelines in your experiments. The staff of the Obama '08 campaign firmly believed that a video was the right choice for the campaign's home page, but in testing, a family photo beat it by a large margin (**Figure 4.4**). Create your own best-practices knowledge about what *actually* works for your website, and, more importantly, what doesn't. You can leave that for your competitors to blindly implement on their website.

Figure 4.4 Dan Siroker, director of analytics for the Obama '08 campaign, challenged the obvious (and most popular amongst the campaign staff) choice of showing a video on the home page with a simple family photo. The photo outperformed the video and the control with a 40.6 percent lift, estimated to be worth $60 million in donations (http://blog.optimizely.com/how-obama-raised-60-million-by-running-an-exp).

37signals founder Jason Fried's mantra while experimenting is, "Destroy all assumptions." Fried realized that the company probably didn't know what works, and to understand that, it would need to test radically different things, and keep iterating and learning (**Figure 4.5**). It has to be said, not many designers are that open-minded when approaching a design project.

Figure 4.5 37signals challenged the usability best-practices guideline of keeping your content above the page fold with a long-form approach that had many page scrolls. It delivered a 37.5 percent lift in net sign-ups compared to the original.

Takeaway

▲ Best practices are a good place to start for experiment ideas.

▲ Don't follow best practices blindly, and don't be afraid to break best practices to put something new on the table.

Usability testing

Traditional usability testing involves several steps: setting up or getting access to a usability lab, recruiting test participants, scheduling test sessions, creating test scripts, conducting the test sessions, consolidating the findings, and then making recommendations.

The challenge for traditional usability recommendations is proving the value. Without quantifiable results, it's hard to show how recommendations will translate into more sales or increased conversion. Running an experiment provides support for the findings of a usability test, and gives quantifiable results.

When your usability sessions are geared toward finding problems and highlighting opportunities, there's huge value to gain from completing occasional usability testing alongside experimenting.

> To identify problems on which to focus,... teams... can take a variety of approaches. Consider a revised workflow that begins with an expert-level heuristic evaluation used in conjunction with informal testing methods, followed by informal and formal testing. More specifically, consider using online tools and paid services to investigate hunches, then use more formal methods to test and validate revised solutions that involve a designer's input.
>
> *"The Myth of Usability Testing," Robert Hoekman Jr., A List Apart 294*

Observed problems

Deciding which of the problems you observe in a usability test are real can be a challenge. It's difficult to tell if the problem a participant tells you about in a usability session, either because she was prompted or because she feels she should say *something*, would stop her from completing her order in a real-world scenario.

To give you the best chance of determining real problems that will make good experiments, observe participants' actions rather than asking for verbal feedback and note where they appear to get lost or hit bumps.

- $1.85 billon dollar customer experience mistake made by Walmart (a conservative estimate of lost revenue that does not include the hundreds of millions spent on remodeling stores).

- Why? Customers answered a Walmart survey and told Walmart that they would prefer less clutter in the stores.

- Saw an immediate loss in sales and decline in same-store sales data.

While customers will say they like cleaner, easier-to-navigate stores (who doesn't?), their behavior shows that even more important to them is a broad selection of low-priced items…. Walmart and other companies have an opportunity to learn an important customer experience lesson: mind the gap between what customers say and what they do.

"Walmart's $1.85 billon dollar mistake," Phil Terry, Daily Artifacts

Useless features

If you can identify features or options that customers don't care about, you can use those opportunities to experiment removing them to free up real estate for something customers will find useful, or for improving visibility to understand whether it adds value with more prominence.

> Besides problems, also observe the things that particpants didn't seem to notice or didn't use at all.

Social game developer wooga uses A/B testing to refine their games on a weekly basis after launch. According to *Wired,* wooga's "core discipline is A/B or split testing, in which new features are introduced to a selection of users, and their reactions measured. Features remain only if users engage with them. If they don't respond, wooga tries new features until they do."

Takeaway

▲ Usability testing still has a role to play; focus on finding problems and opportunities to feed into your experiments pipeline.

▲ Shape experiments to deliver a user experience that feeds into the bigger picture.

5

On Design

Design for design's sake

As designers, we're passionate about what we create. We'll very happily spend time reworking something, changing something, improving something. Give any designer a design and he'll think of something to do to it. If you ask what he's trying to achieve, you might find the answer is he's designing just for the love of doing it.

We've already talked about perfection getting in the way of shipping experiments, and it's worth reiterating here: it's crucial to find the point where a design, though not perfect, is good enough.

> Good design keeps the user happy, the manufacturer in the black and the aesthete unoffended.
>
> *Raymond Loewy*

What are you trying to improve?

There's no point in designing solutions to problems that don't exist. Experiments help you focus on areas where your website can make more money. Whatever design you're working on, be clear about what you're trying to achieve and ensure that testing can show it will add value to the site.

Why is it actually better?

Keep in mind that existing customers are used to your current website. Unless you make it better in some way, why would you expect them to like it more than what they have already?

Avoid vanity projects, that is, imposing your own design preferences that aren't clearly better for customers (**Figure 5.1**). Chances are, if you don't know why it's better, your customers won't either.

Courtesy Kai Hendry on Flickr

Figure 5.1 This keyboard is a good example of design for the sake of design, with plenty of unnecessary features; you'll notice it even has a turbo button!

Takeaway

▲ Don't design for the sake of it. Understand what you're trying to improve and why it's actually better for your customers.

Emotions and expectations

You've spent lots of time thinking about the new design and making it right. You're excited about running the experiment and you're sure it's going to be a good win. But when you run the experiment, the design turns out to be worse than the control. Your customers have told you they don't like it. That can be a big letdown.

Emotional attachment

As a designer, if you're passionate about your craft, it's hard not to get emotionally attached to the things you create. It's disappointing and even exhausting when something you created so clearly demonstrates that it has no value.

Your design preferences can hinder your experiments. It's hard to commit to a favorite then have to continually devise experiments to defend it.

Be open to what did work, even if it wasn't what you consider the best design. When the winner is not what you expected or wanted, that's even more reason to explore what works about it. Your customers have told you what they think. Listen and adapt.

> You can't improve a design when you're emotionally attached to previous decisions. Improvements come from flexibility and openness.
>
> *Ryan Singer, Signal vs. Noise, the 37signals blog*

Designer expectations

We tend to value our own ideas more than other people's ideas. Behavioral economist Dan Ariely identified something he calls the

"Not-Invented-Here Bias." Similarly, when we construct products ourselves, we overvalue them—this is known as the "IKEA Effect."

Other people may bring you ideas that will produce bigger results than
your own. Be careful not to miss them because you thought your idea
was better just because it was yours.

> Verna was a front-desk clerk at one of the dorms. She was respon-
> sible for helping students if a problem came up and used [my
> software] to get her job done...
>
> One day while fixing the the front-desk computer I asked Verna,
> "What do you think of [it]?" She immediately supplied a laundry list
> of complaints. It didn't work well, it was confusing, she never knew
> where to go or what to do, and so forth.
>
> It would have been easy to blame her. Maybe she just needed better
> training or maybe she wasn't trying hard enough. But that was all
> ego: I was just upset because she told me the product I helped build
> was pretty awful.
>
> Her critique was absolutely fair. I had built solutions I liked for
> problems I wasn't even sure existed.
>
> *"What Verna Taught Me," Jesse Farmer, 20bits.com*

Design decisions won't always go your way. There will always be things
that add value to your website that you just don't like.

Be passionate about your work, but be committed to delivering design
that delivers value.

Takeaway

▲ Don't let emotional attachment to experiment designs
influence what you test next.

▲ Be passionate about your craft, but be committed to
experimenting and learning.

Competitor bias

Most businesses have a competitor they aspire to be like, and they over-estimate that competitor's knowledge of website design. The assumption is that whatever is on the competitor's website, "it must be good and we should be doing it too."

> You might be surprised to learn that the competition probably knows nothing more about its website's influences than you do (or maybe less, since you're reading a book on experiments!).

It might also surprise you that what works for the competition likely won't work for you. Your site, user experience, traffic sources, conversion rates, pricing, brand trust, and positioning are different. So even in nearly identical competing businesses, there's little chance that blindly copying features or design out of context will give you success.

Rather than copying competitor ideas, come up with a hypothesis of what you think is adding value for them about this design or feature, and build an experiment for your business around it.

Takeaway

▲ Rather than blindly copying competitors, take inspiration from them to build experiment hypotheses for your business.

Design by committee

When you put experimenting at the heart of your design process and judge your own ideas on their objective merits, it's easy to give the same consideration to other people's ideas. This habit will stand you in good stead when it comes time to deal with the stakeholder committee. Michael Arrington, founder and former coeditor of TechCrunch, put it nicely: "When there are too many cooks in the kitchen all you get is a mess."

> The iPhone is clearly a vision of a single core team, or maybe even one man. It happened to be a good dream, and that device now dominates mobile culture. But it's extremely unlikely Apple would have ever built it if they conducted lots of focus groups and customer outreach first.
>
> *"Digg's Biggest Problem Is Its Users And Their Constant Opinions On Things,"*
> *Michael Arrington, TechCrunch*

If you're unfamiliar with design by committee, here's how it goes: You present a design to a few stakeholders or business owners, control of the design is lost, solutions are devised on the fly by a combination of everyone's opinions or by the loudest voice in the room, and you're left to clean up what comes out the other end.

The HiPPO can't be ignored

Experimenters have a term to describe a design process that's directed by the loudest voice: they say it's driven by the HiPPO (highest-paid person's opinion).

You've no doubt experienced this many times: the most senior stakeholder decides almost exclusively the direction the design will take; the appropriate skill set or design merit to determine the direction is not required.

Avinash Kaushik, Google analytics evangelist and author of *Web Analytics 2.0,* makes it pretty clear that you, not the HiPPO, need to determine the direction of your experiments: "Most websites suck because HiPPOs create them."

As an experimenter, you try to avoid bias toward your own ideas and judge each design purely on the proven value it brings to the business. Unless stakeholders can bring a unique business perspective, their feedback is as that of a customer—they have no better view on what makes a good design than you do.

> Design is often thought of as a superficial add-on, but the objective approach and measurable results of experimenting can boost its credibility.

Quantifying the user experience

There's one very good reason to start experimenting your user experience work: to quantify its value. Running an experiment is the only way to put a cash value on the design changes you make to a website.

This can be a difficult decision. It's easy to make recommendations when they're not measured and valued; it's altogether more difficult to make recommendations when you know it's an experiment that will have a value associated.

But take the losses with the wins. If you don't experiment, you won't know (and can't prove) if you're adding value to the bottom line. Prove the value of your work through experiments, and things like your salary negotiations become a lot easier.

Supporting design decisions

As a UX designer or someone interested in user experience, you've probably suffered through a few stakeholder reviews of your concepts and wireframes, and found that after incorporating the stakeholders' feedback and ideas, your concept was no longer the great user experience you had envisaged.

Similarly, you've probably worked on a project where you knew you could improve the experience, but that wasn't part of the creative brief or the project scope. Maybe you've even had to add a feature that you knew would have a negative impact on the user experience.

Experiments give you the capacity to withstand all that. If you believe there's a better way that your customers will respond to more positively, you'll find it easier to propose an experiment than to encourage stakeholders to simply follow your recommendation.

Experiments let you accept requests, feedback, and ideas and compare them to your own vision of how the experience should be.

Present experiments, not ideas

It seems nothing is easier to kill than a good idea. In his brilliant book *The Myths of Innovation,* Scott Berkun highlights common phrases used for thoughtless idea rejection. These are used by people who have no useful criticism or direction to give, or who choose to dismiss an idea because they don't consider the source to be capable of producing good ideas. You might be familiar with a few of these:

▶ We tried that already.

▶ We've never done that before.

▶ We don't do it that way here.

▶ That never works.

▶ People won't like it.

▶ It's out of scope.

▶ We don't have time.

▶ It's not in our budget.

The list goes on. However, there's an easy way to protect ideas: simply present them as experiments complete with test plans, each with a hypothesis and goal as described in Chapter 1, "On Experimenting." The completeness—and the fact that you're presenting a plan, not just an idea—will help reduce opinion-based requests to modify your designs, and make it much more difficult for stakeholders to reject ideas entirely.

> Couldn't testing help you protect a potential breakthrough from the "fear of stupid"? Absolutely. And if you can't exactly prove that a concept will work, you can at least turn a wild guess into an educated one, and give your collaborators enough confidence to proceed.
>
> *Marty Neumeier,* The Brand Gap

If a stakeholder is concerned or nervous about an experiment design, remind them that it's just an experiment, and the results of that experiment will reveal whether it's the right design decision.

If you're concerned that something a stakeholder has proposed will introduce a negative, you can suggest running an experiment. It's hard to refuse a simple request aimed at proving the value of the idea.

Experiments make meetings irrelevant

At the *New York Times,* staff used to sit around a table trying to decide the best headlines for an important story. Now they simply run all the proposed headlines in an experiment and let readers decide by what they click on. When the winner is determined, it's rolled out to capture the full audience.

Over time, when you deliver experiment results, even the most uneasy stakeholders will become more comfortable with experimenting and interfere less with your approach. When it's time to demonstrate the value of your designs, use your results to help stakeholders understand that for experiment success, it's in their interest to have emotional distance from the individual experiment designs. We'll talk more about results in Chapter 8, "On Results."

Takeaway

▲ Use experiments to show the value of your work and to continually learn and improve your skill set.

▲ Use experiments to evaluate others' design requests objectively.

▲ Reduce stakeholder interference by presenting test plans rather than ideas.

▲ Demonstrate that the approach you use delivers results to get stakeholders on board, avoid design by committee, and prevent the HiPPO from deciding the direction.

6

On Ideas

Data-driven ideas

You'll probably have many data sources in your business: qualitative and quantitative, online, and maybe even offline.

But having access to data is only half the story. The real challenge and opportunity is how you interpret that data into actionable insights for your optimization efforts. Let's look more closely at a few of the best data sources for drawing out good experiment ideas.

Optimization

No change is too small in the right context, in the right place in your customer journey, and for the right buying mentality of your customer. You may be beguiled by the idea of a major redesign, but don't rule out subtle nudges that can have a noticeable impact.

Some elements on your website will have more influence than others. Simple refinements on these could deliver big wins with little effort right off, and continue to deliver results as you improve further. Through your experiment results, website analytics, and usability testing, you can identify the areas of your site that most influence customers, and develop ideas that challenge them to do even better.

> If you have some pages on a site which are critical to its overall success, instigate a program of A/B split testing. You cannot afford to guess; you have to know.
>
> *"Design Choices Can Cripple a Website," Nick Usborne, A List Apart 207*

Website analytics

Accessing analytics for your website's key performance indicators is relatively easy. Almost every online business has some form of analytics, from the free Google Analytics to enterprise tools like Adobe SiteCatalyst, Coremetrics, or Webtrends. Analytics are a great resource for finding areas of opportunity on your site.

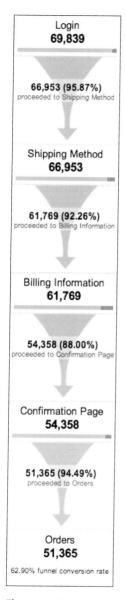

Where to find conversion opportunities in your website analytics

▶ **Funnel analysis** Analyze your purchase funnel start to end and look for the areas with the highest abandonment (**Figure 6.1**).

▶ **Form analysis** Forms are always tricky for customers. Try to identify any form fields that are giving customers problems.

▶ **Path analysis** Identify where customers go next from your key pages or steps. If it's not where you want them to be, figure out why they are distracted.

▶ **Bounce rates** Analyze pages where your customers aren't engaged and are leaving the site and consider ways to improve the pages.

▶ **Page conversion** Compare low- and high-converting pages. Understand the differences that could be driving differing performance by page.

▶ **Session reply/heat maps** Observe where customers are clicking, how far they're scrolling, and what elements are attracting their attention. Consider whether this is where you want them to focus.

Figure 6.1 Web analytics will help you identify areas to focus on. In this checkout funnel example, you can see that an opportunity exists on the billing information page, as customers are having the most trouble completing this step.

Qualitative data

As you observe existing problems, you and your team can design improvements to be tested. The desire for optimization—improving what already exists—often spurs experiment ideas that return big wins.

> Data obtained from qualitative sources, such as usability testing, about how your site is performing right now or has performed historically is full of insights that can launch ideas.

If you're just getting started with experiments, there are probably obvious problems on your website that you can get big wins from right away. But after you've dealt with the obvious ones and fully exploited your website analytics, a usability session might just provide a wide-open funnel to gather observations about hidden issues.

Usability reports

Jeff Sauro, author of *A Practical Guide to Measuring Usability,* recommends giving each usability problem a name, a description, and a severity rating.

Severity ratings of observed usability problems

1. Prevents task completion
2. Causes significant delay or frustration
3. Has a relatively minor impact on frustration
4. Is a suggestion

When reviewing qualitative data from usability reports, focus your experiment efforts on items that have the highest severity ratings. Fixing these problems is a good idea and solutions shouldn't be hard to find.

Other qualitative sources

You can find ideas in other qualitative data, such as exit surveys, customer feedback questionnaires, or customer satisfaction scores. If your business has a call centre, try listening in on some customer calls to get ideas on how to satisfy them online. All this qualitative information can be a source of good experiment ideas.

Experiments data

Experiments quickly become data sources themselves. Observing the reaction to a change you implemented in a controlled test is the best way to reveal insights, gaps, and opportunities to increase website conversion.

> Team Analytics was the Obama campaign's watchdog, monitoring and measuring everything from the effectiveness of online ads, to the open rates of emails. Using services like Google Analytics and Google Website Optimizer, the campaign gathered enough data to establish a solid understanding of where supporters were spending their time on the Obama site, and where and when to place the ads that would draw them there. ...Improvements and adjustments were made daily and the results could be seen in the improved conversion rates.
>
> ...While many companies are not dealing with the condensed and finite timeline of an election, there is much to be learned from constantly testing and updating processes.
>
> *Jeff Lane in* Yes We Did *by Rahaf Harfoush*

As you accumulate data from experiments, keep records to help inform and inspire future experiment ideas. It's a good idea to bring your experiment data, results, and learning into a knowledge base or a wiki alongside your experiment ideas.

We'll look more at experiment data in Chapter 7, "On Analysis."

Takeaway

▲ Use all the data sources available to you to drive out action ideas for experimenting.

▲ Remember that data sources help you identify the problems that exist on your website right now, which you can improve in an experiment.

Innovative ideas

You'll reach a point in your optimization efforts where it becomes harder to get winners, and you'll feel that you've reached an optimal level for the current experience. Now we'll look at breaking away from that by experimenting original ideas.

The unknown

It's important to keep some experiment capacity for innovation, to avoid wasting time on improving something that exists when it could be much better if you threw it away and started again.

Innovation really comes into focus when you reach a natural saturation point in your experimenting, where you feel that what you have today has been optimized as far as it can be. This is demonstrated in **Figure 6.2**; the low peak (known as the local maximum) represents the point in which you've hit the limit of the current design. It's as effective as it's ever going to be on its current structural foundation—it's optimized. The high peak represents something better (known as the global maximum), which you can only reach through innovating.

Where optimization is improving what already exists, innovation is trying something truly unknown, that doesn't exist today, and that data can't help you determine.

You won't know how good or bad these ideas are until you try an experiment. Scott Berkun summarizes innovation perfectly, comparing it to exploration: "Like Captain Cook, you can't find something new if you limit your travels to places others have already found."

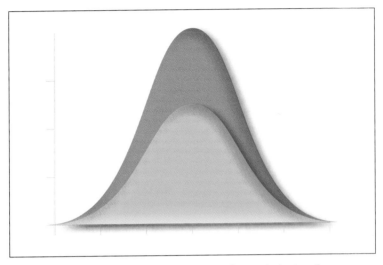

Figure 6.2 The low peak represents the local maximum, the best performance you can achieve from your current design. The high peak represents the global maximum, which requires innovation to reach.

Intuition

While working on Burbn (a mobile app that let users check in at locations, make plans, earn points, post pictures, and more) CEO Kevin Systrom and the cofounders made the intuitive decision that posting pictures was the best opportunity. Focused on that single purpose, they cut everything in the Burbn app except for its photo, comment, and like capabilities. What remained became Instagram and the rest is history.

When you want to innovate, following hunches is crucial for uncovering new ideas and opportunities. It may seem like a contradiction to experiment using both scientific methods and intuition, but you need to capture both to give you a wider range. There are no methods to follow to understand if a hunch is a good idea; you have to experiment.

> Prof. Gerd Gigerenzer, the director of the Max Planck Institute for Human Development in Berlin,... has developed the startling claim that intuition makes our decisions not just quicker but better. He rejects the notion that hunches are second best.
>
> *"When Less is More," Matt Ridley*

Consider every idea as a valid experiment idea, even if you've never seen it before, can't find any data or research to support it, and really have no direction on whether or not it has value. Running an experiment will tell you.

You won't always find a winner from an experiment that followed a hunch, but you'll certainly learn, be inspired with new ideas, and perhaps connect with other ideas and learnings to make something valuable in future. But most importantly, by following hunches and making intuitive decisions, you have a shot at your own Instagram moments.

Connections

As Steve Jobs famously said, "Creativity is just connecting things." Ideas by their very nature are connective. The more you experiment, the more ideas, theories, and hypotheses you'll have to test.

You won't remember all the ideas you had, all the thoughts about why an experiment behaved a certain way, or all the next things you plan to do at some time in future.

Write ideas down. It sounds simple, but it's crucial. Start building a wiki or collection (**Figure 6.3**) of all your test results, the things you discovered, and any ideas you think need further exploration.

Then bring together stories about your visitors' experiences. Review and read them frequently. Often an idea you captured in the past that wasn't quite fully formed will make absolute sense when connected with something new.

Figure 6.3 Evernote is a perfect tool for capturing and archiving experiment ideas, results, learning, and anything else that can inspire you to experiment.

> The creative process requires more than reason. Most original thinking isn't even verbal. It requires "a groping experimentation with ideas, governed by intuitive hunches and inspired by the unconscious."
>
> *David Ogilvy*, Confessions of an Advertising Man

Continuous innovation

Remember, experimenting is a continuous process—so too is innovation. When approaching innovative experiments, be prepared to fail and be motivated to iterate and try again.

Failure is simply part of the process. To find winners you need to be open to and encourage failure.

Fail fast where possible, so you learn as much as you can from the least development and experiment capacity you can. You'll need the capacity to react and keep trying.

Whereas traditional product development would involve making product decisions using business intuition and knowledge, Zynga turned decision-making on its head by hypothesis-driven product testing, quick analysis and agile roll-out based on how customers behaved. This agile, data-driven test-and-learn methodology enabled Zynga to roll out new features every 24 hours, a previously unheard-of release frequency.

"What is your organization's Analytics Maturity?," Piyanka Jain, Forbes

Takeaway

▲ Introduce innovation in your experiments, especially as finding winners gets harder.

▲ Keep a wiki or knowledge base of all your learnings to allow future discovery of new ideas.

Design-inspired ideas

We live in a world of brilliant ideas. New products and services continually change customer expectations. Let's look at some elements of everyday design that you can observe and react to in your experiments.

Social networks

Many experimenters look to competitive businesses for ideas; you've probably done this many times already. But have you ever looked at the social networks to be inspired?

Think about it. Social networks like Facebook and Twitter are engrained in your customers' lives. These sites get a lot more use than your site or your competitors' sites. Interactions people find on Facebook will not be unfamiliar to them.

Don't copy blindly, but look at how social networks handle situations like forms, interactions, and updates—features visitors use over and over. A new feature on Facebook can replace a best practice overnight. A new feature on your competitor's site will probably remain new for a long time.

Popular devices

When Apple launched the iPhone, the industry changed. Since the introduction of the iPad, the mobile and tablet market has boomed. Right now, up to 20 percent of all traffic to your site is likely from mobile devices.

Take inspiration from popular products, the design of the devices, the interactions, and the interfaces (**Figure 6.4**). Your customers are using these everyday devices more than your website. Experiment with the features and details they love .

Figure 6.4 Loren Brichter, the developer behind Tweetie (later acquired by Twitter to become the official Twitter app), invented the hugely popular pull-to-refresh gesture. It became a best practice and expected feature instantly, making its way into countless iOS apps and mobile-optimized websites.

Design best practice

We already looked at best practices in Chapter 4, "On UX," but it's worth reiterating here that best-practice design remains a valuable source of ideas for experiments.

Continue to test accepted and evolving best-practices guidelines in your experiments. While best practices can seem a little boring and not particularly inspiring compared to some of the new things you'll be exploring, don't be surprised when the usual and familiar beats the new and interesting.

Offline ideas

Aad Kieboom directs Amsterdam's Schiphol airport expansion. He came up with an idea and, with his staff, conducted an unusual experiment. He etched a black housefly in each urinal in the men's toilets. A simple hypothesis: you see a target, you aim at it. Aad was right: the fly etching reduced splash by 80 percent. A subtle design nudge that focuses attention and changes behavior.

This is just one example of innovative and persuasive offline everyday design. In airports, hotels, shopping malls, bookstores, banks, and restaurants, you'll encounter things designed to persuade you. Consider anything interesting you see offline as inspiration for your next experiment.

Real-life explorations

Everything you experience in life brings insights you can use in your testing program. I wanted to learn more about mobile and the App Store, so I created an app to explore. Upon release, with acclaim on leading websites like Lifehacker.com, it reached the top 25 in the App Store for Paid Productivity apps. Exploring what was a new area for me brought valuable insights—it taught me the challenges of gestural interactions, the value of positive reviews for App Store rankings, and the limitations of app data and analysis. Exploration and discovery are part of the creative process. Lessons and ideas don't have to be directly transferable to be useful. Try things beyond the subject matter and your areas of expertise; allow your everyday explorations to bring new perspectives (**Figure 6.5**).

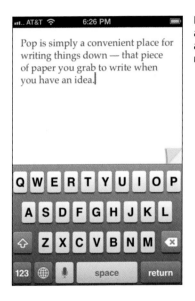

Figure 6.5 Pop for iOS, an app I made to get experience and to learn more about mobile and the App Store.

Takeaway

▲ Take inspiration from popular social networks and devices in your experiments.

▲ Be inspired by good ideas you encounter offline too.

New associations and fresh ideas are more likely to come out of a varied store of memories and experience than out of a collection that is all of one kind.

W. I. B. Beveridge

Shared ideas

To get the most from your experiments you need to harness the combined knowledge and skills of your entire organization. Here we'll look at some ways to ensure that the best ideas are coming forward.

Work together

Arch West, the inventor of Doritos, was vice president of marketing for Frito-Lay. He and David Pace, the inventor of Pace picante sauce, realized that if they displayed their products together, they'd both sell more.

You could run your experiments on your own and get some wins, but like West and Pace, if you share ideas with others and let them combine their expertise with yours, your experiment efforts will bear a lot more fruit.

Experiment programs often lean toward either the creative or the scientific side, depending on where the experiment team sits within the business. Welcome collaborators with a wide range of approaches so you can use the combined strengths of your business to drive both scientific and artistic creativity in your experiments.

> If you have an apple and I have an apple and we exchange apples then you and I will still each have one apple. But if you have an idea and I have an idea and we exchange these ideas, then each of us will have two ideas.
>
> *George Bernard Shaw*

Get people on board

How do you get people on board so they share ideas and become committed to experimenting long term?

Share common goals

Every stakeholder has different priorities, responsibilities, opinions, and preferences, but chances are most of them will have the same overriding goal. It's probably the same goal you defined as the success measure of your experiment.

Remind stakeholders that you share the same goal and invite their input and ideas up front. This will help keep your experiments focused on proven ideas rather than on people's pet ideas and cottage industries.

> When it's time to report results, you may face less resistance if you got buy-in up front.

Share credit for ideas

You'll be running the experiments and maybe distributing the results too. You'll quickly become the face of experiments and, by association, you'll be credited with experiment successes and responsible for failures—whether they are your ideas or not.

Remember to recognize the work others contributed or the ideas they shared to give you the result. Appreciate and reward their contributions. Sharing credit for ideas is the best way to win your colleagues' continued commitment to experimenting.

Takeaway

▲ Work together with others in your business to ensure sharing of ideas.

▲ Get people on board by sharing common goals and credit for ideas and results.

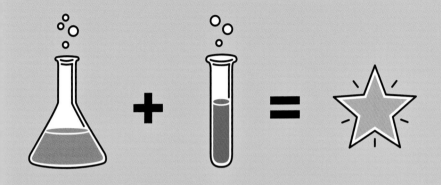

PART III

Moving Forward

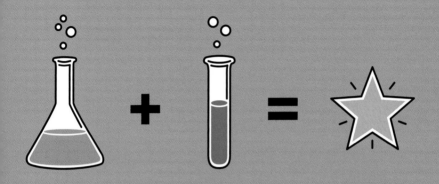

7

On Analysis

Trusting your findings

Understanding the results of your experiments can be a complicated affair. Luckily, there are a few simple methods to make sense of all the data your experiments accumulate and give you confidence in your findings.

Statistical significance

In your experiments, you attempt to hold all variables constant except the thing you want to investigate. The reality, of course, is that many variables are not constant. You're comparing similar groups, but those groups themselves will have differences that introduce noise. That's where statistical significance comes in (**Figure 7.1**).

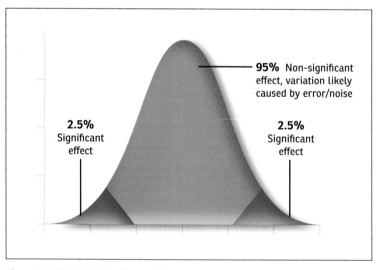

95% Non-significant effect, variation likely caused by error/noise

2.5% Significant effect

2.5% Significant effect

Figure 7.1 Statistical significance illustrated.

Statistical significance measures how confident you can be that the difference you observe in your experiment is not due to chance events or random error in data-gathering. In experiments, 95 percent significance is generally used as the threshold, ensuring there is only a low probability that the result is chance or random noise (**Figure 7.2**).

Confidence isn't on a time axis that ensures it gets higher over time, it moves around with the natural performance variances seen during your experiment, likely coming in and out of confidence many times. It's important not to simply react the first time your experiment hits 95 percent, but instead let your experiment finish, and consider the confidence of your experiment for the entire duration.

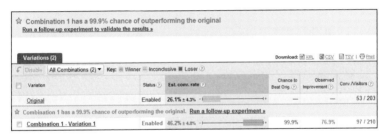

Figure 7.2 Different tools name the significance level differently. Google Website Optimizer, for example, uses a much more friendly "Chance to beat original."

So if your experiment has reached 95 percent confidence or above, you can accept it as a winner. There is still a 5 percent probability that your result was caused by chance, but you can accept this, safe in the knowledge that as you run many experiments, your outcome will be right most of the time.

Be careful with experiment results that never reach 95 percent confidence (**Figure 7.3**), as it's increasingly likely that you're reacting to mere noise in your experiment.

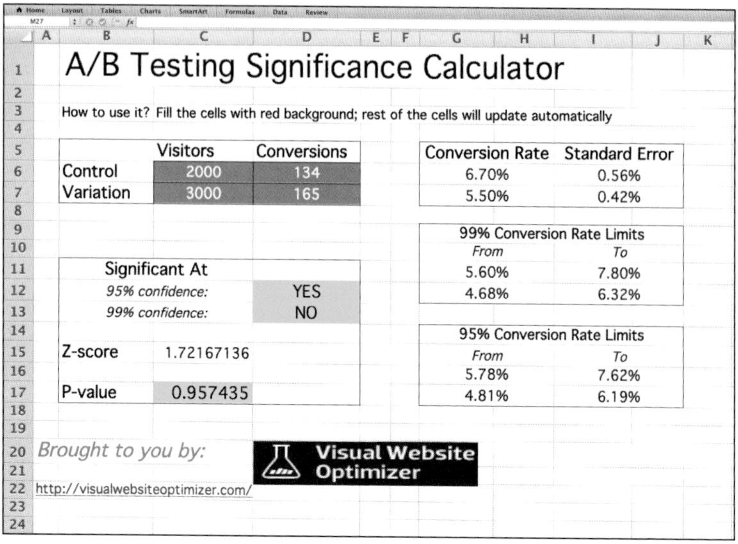

A/B Testing Significance Calculator

How to use it? Fill the cells with red background; rest of the cells will update automatically

	Visitors	Conversions
Control	2000	134
Variation	3000	165

	Conversion Rate	Standard Error
	6.70%	0.56%
	5.50%	0.42%

Significant At

| 95% confidence: | YES |
| 99% confidence: | NO |

| Z-score | 1.72167136 |
| P-value | 0.957435 |

99% Conversion Rate Limits	
From	To
5.60%	7.80%
4.68%	6.32%

95% Conversion Rate Limits	
From	To
5.78%	7.62%
4.81%	6.19%

Brought to you by: **Visual Website Optimizer**

http://visualwebsiteoptimizer.com/

Figure 7.3 Vendor systems calculate statistical significance for you. If you're using your own tool, Visual Website Optimizer offers a simple calculator that helps you discover whether your experiment has reached an acceptable significance level.

Stabilization, standard deviation, and outliers

While statistical significance is the most reliable measure to understand the validity of results, it isn't enough to ensure that your experiment is a winner. It's also good practice to look for stabilization (the experiment difference appears to be relatively stable over time), standard deviation (the measure of how much variation from the average there is in the data to determine how narrowly or widely the results are likely to vary), and outliers (any large, atypical events that could impact the overall performance; for example, in one day it just so happened that two people made huge orders that rocketed average order value, and both happened to be in your challenger variant).

"Outlier" is a scientific term to describe things or phenomena that lie outside normal experience. In the summer, in Paris, we expect most days to be somewhere between warm and very hot. But imagine if you had a day in the middle of August where the temperature fell below freezing. That day would be outlier.

"What is Outliers *about?," Malcolm Gladwell*

Takeaway

▲ Ensure that your experiment results are unlikely to be attributable to random chance.

▲ Measure how much variance there is and whether it's steady.

▲ Look for atypical external conditions that could have affected your data.

Segmentation

As you run your experiment and keep an eye on your dashboard, you'll notice that visitors can be divided into groups by certain shared characteristics, such as how frequently they use the site or what device they are on. Segmenting your results is all about understanding what drove the positive performance in your experiences, and discovering new opportunities for experimentation in the next wave.

If you focus on the right characteristics, segmentation can be an enormous help in analyzing and understanding your data.

In results that are flat or negative, perhaps you'll identify what area prevented the experiment from otherwise producing a winner.

> There is no KPI so insightful all by itself, even in a trend or against a forecast, that it can't be made more impactful by applying segmentation.
>
> *"Excellent Analytics Tip#2: Segment Absolutely Everything," Avinash Kaushik, Occam's Razor*

Slice and dice your results by segment

▶ **New/Repeat** This is the segment you should look into for every experiment. New customers will often behave differently from your existing customers, as they have different expectations, experiences, and intentions when visiting your site. You'll find opportunities here for targeting and tailoring the experience for new and repeat customer behavior.

▶ **Device** As mobile web sessions continue to grow, it's increasingly important to break down your results by the top devices your visitors use. For example, understand whether your experiment performed as well for iPad traffic as it did for desktop, and identify opportunities to optimize for mobile.

▶ **Channel** Break down by channel to understand your experiment performance by paid (Google pay-per-click ads), natural (search engine listings), direct (visited your website by typing the URL into the browser), affiliate, or other (social media like Facebook or Twitter) traffic. You may find that a result that was flat or negative overall was actually really good for a specific channel.

▶ **Browser** From time to time, cross-browser issues with features will show up in your experiments. Break down your results by browser type so that if a browser-specific issue is discovered, it won't skew all your data or lead you to a wrong conclusion.

▶ **Time/Day/Season** You'll probably notice differing performance in your experiments during the week and on the weekend. Break down your results in appropriate timeframes to factor in the "weekend effect." Seasonality will also play a role. For example, if your business sells cards, your activity will go up around the holidays.

Or if you are a retailer, you'll no doubt have most of your demand in the "golden quarter," the lead-up to Christmas.

▶ **Product** If your website offers differing product or service categories, break down your results to understand if your experiment drove the same behavior for each, and identify areas to improve.

Swimming in data

If you don't know what you're looking for, you'll certainly find something in your results. Whether it's relevant to your experiment is another thing.

> If you don't know where you are going, any road will take you there.
>
> *Lewis Carroll*

Collecting data is easy

It's easy to collect data on how visitors use your website, and the cost of collecting as much data as possible is little to nothing. This vast amount of data can be subdivided into almost limitless categories in the search for meaningful relationships. But that doesn't mean all that data is always useful, and more importantly, it doesn't mean all that data is relevant to your experiment.

Not all data is useful

We just looked at some useful segments, but consider whether those segments are relevant to your particular experiment. You could probably segment your experiment further, but before you cut your data too many ways consider whether it will have any real value.

Here's an hypothetical (and exaggerated) example: you could show how your experiment performed on a rainy Wednesday evening among women shoppers who visited via the site via Facebook on their iPhones. Not a particularly useful insight (unless you are in the umbrella business and offer good deals on a Wednesday).

It's tempting to go beyond your primary goal and highlight interesting observations you stumbled upon in your data somewhere, but keep in mind that with data, if you are looking for anything you will find something.

That looks interesting

When you uncover something interesting, question whether it's really relevant to your experiment. Keep in mind Twyman's law: "Any figure that looks interesting or different is usually wrong." Avoid drowning in data. Focus on the experiment's impact on the key performance indicators (KPIs) you defined as important in your test plan.

Takeaway

▲ Segment your results to learn what works and to identify new opportunities to experiment.

▲ Focus on the KPIs you defined as the success factors for your experiment and avoid swimming in data.

Data cleanliness

We just discussed swimming in data, but before you even get into the pool, it's a good idea to make sure the data is clean. Here are a few things to look out for that can seriously tamper with your experiment results.

Internal traffic

It's likely your business will have lots of internal visitors who will also be exposed to your experiments, but whose experience could actually affect your results and outcome. For example:

▶ Quality assurance testing teams may be running scripts to measure website technical performance or response times. That traffic would appear in your experiment data.

▶ Call center or support staff may be using the website in their jobs, adding noise to the results as they visit many times during the same experiment.

▶ Performance or session-capture systems may be generating traffic that adds noise by constantly trolling through your website.

If your business has many staff members who are also customers and who shop on your business website while at work, you may not want to exclude those customers entirely from your experiments (after all, they are paying customers too and you'll want to understand the impact), but do at least segment the results to understand if the differing nature of these internal customers adds noise to your results.

Robots and spiders

A surprising amount of your site traffic is "non-normal," that is, not generated by real people. Consider search engines, robots, spiders, and any other kind of traffic crawling your site at any given time, originating from your own tools, like site speed/uptime measuring systems or competitors' tools, like price-scraping systems.

All this non-normal, junk traffic could have an impact on your experiment results. If you can, make your results cleaner by identifying and excluding non-normal traffic from your experiments. You can do this either by skipping it during data gathering via some sort of script magic, or by stripping it out before data analysis.

Takeaway

⚠ Customers and potential customers are not the only visitors generating traffic on your site.

⚠ Make your results as clean as you can by removing non-normal traffic.

Timing

Primacy effect

Primacy effect is observed when a change that proves to be better over time temporarily degrades performance to begin with. Perhaps your experiment offered a new navigation structure or a new checkout experience, and your repeat visitors, who are familiar with the old design, take a little while to get used to the new design. New customers, unfamiliar with your website and so coming with no learned behavior, will give you a somewhat less biased view.

Primacy effect can cause you to draw incorrect conclusions, so it's important to look out for it. A simple way to understand whether the primacy effect may be holding back an experiment is to segment your results by new/repeat customers and see if new customers behaved differently.

Of course, the primacy effect can't be used as a scapegoat for variants your existing customers simply don't like. If you feel it is holding back an experiment that could be a winner, run the experiment longer and observe whether performance improves over time. If it doesn't, it isn't a primacy effect. Your repeat customers simply like the old design better, and you'd best consider sticking with it.

Newness effect

Similar to the primacy effect, but with the opposite outcome, is the "newness effect." The newness effect is usually observed in less solid goals, like click-through rates, and is caused by customers clicking on or interacting with the new thing simply because it is new and they want to explore.

You could wrongly assume all this increased activity in your experiment challenger means your new feature is a success, when in fact customers could have checked it out, realized it had no value for them, and didn't use it next time.

Again the solution is to test over a longer period of time. Is the new feature still driving the same behavior and getting the same use on the second, third, or fourth visits? Is it still used as heavily after one week or one month?

Weekend effect and seasonality

Your customers probably behave differently on your website during different trading periods or conditions, like weekday versus weekend, sale season versus traditional full-price trading, or peak trading versus normal seasonal trading. Without even considering experiments, you can observe weekend or seasonal effects on performance in your website analytics.

> It's important to consider weekend effect and seasonality, to ensure that you learn if your experiment works during a specific condition, or all the time.

Run every experiment at least through the weekend, and consider carefully the seasonality aspect of your results.

The best way to learn about seasonality is, of course, to experiment through different seasons. For example, experiment to see if winners behave the same during peak—for example, when customers are in a rush to buy their Christmas presents—and vice versa. Or test how your experiments perform when customers are buying items during a sale against the more relaxed and considered behavior you can expect during full-price trading season.

Takeaway

▲ Look out for effects that could cause you to draw the wrong conclusions from your experiment.

▲ Take timing from both the customer and business standpoints into account when analyzing data.

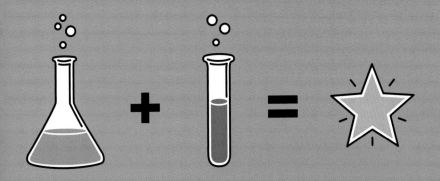

8

On Results

Create a clear message

Now that you have a thorough understanding of your experiment results, it's time to share them with others. The real challenge and opportunity is how you interpret data from your tests into insights for your optimization efforts. Experiment results that are unnecessarily complicated lead to inaction. It's crucial that you translate what you've learnt from the experiment into a clear, actionable outcome. Here we'll look at how to create a clear message to share with others and affect change.

Results

Key to creating a clear message is a consistent approach to communicating the results of your experiments. In Chapter 1, "On Experimenting," we described three goals: improve, protect, and make no difference. In alignment with those, here are three results you can use to describe the experiment outcome: significant benefit, detrimental impact, and no difference. It's as simple as that—use these as your results headline, and add extra commentary if necessary. Let's look at each result a little more closely.

Significant benefit

You've found a result that is statistically significant and proved empirically that it adds value to your business. Well done! You proved your hypothesis to be correct. This is an easy result to communicate. Quite simply:

> "The challenger represents a significant benefit to the business."

It's worth noting you could find results that are significant, but still aren't worth implementing, for example if the cost of implementing the feature is more than the value it adds.

Detrimental impact

You've found a result that you're confident would be detrimental to your business. This is disappointing, but consider that you've saved your business money by preventing a bad design decision from going live.

Negative results can be harder to communicate, as you'll likely have a rationale for what went wrong (rather than just confirming your hypothesis, as happens with a winner). Still, ensure that the result is clear with a headline:

> "The challenger would introduce a detrimental impact to the business."

No difference

A likely outcome for any experiment is that it's flat, that is, it makes no difference at all. You'll see this often when you're just starting out (as you become braver), and when you've already found many winners (when you need to extend your reach).

The result headline should be clear and unbiased since you have no evidence to drive an outcome:

> "This challenger makes no significantly measurable impact to the business."

Some discussion of the details is crucial when your experiment is flat. Perhaps your hypothesis was "make no difference" and you've just proved it. If it's an existing feature, you've proved that it adds no value and can be removed. Perhaps a new idea has no influence on your customers, or perhaps you simply need to try again with a more drastically different design.

How worried should we be that the feature we thought improved our product actually does nothing, or worse, hurts our bottom line? How can we ever really know that we're making the correct decision? And is it better to run tests more quickly or more accurately?

The answers to these questions depend on the cost of a bad decision. If mistakes are cheap then it's better to make 1,000 decisions and get only 60% of them right than to make 100 decisions and get 100% of them right...

If you have millions of customers, like Google or Amazon, a 1% improvement to the bottom line is a huge win. Conversely, a 1% mistake is a huge hit.

"Speed vs Certainty in A/B Testing," Jesse Farmer, 20bits.com

Monetize your results

While a clear outcome is great, what people really care about is value. You can communicate the value as a percentage, for example, "10 percent lift in revenue," but percentages are difficult to understand without knowing the area of the site that was tested, the current conversion rates, the traffic, and so forth.

There's a better way. Monetize your experiment results by giving an incremental annual revenue figure. It's concrete and tangible, and you'll have no trouble getting buy-in for experiments when you can demonstrate it. Everyone gets it.

There are many ways to monetize your results, applying as much rigor as you feel is necessary. You could create a ballpark figure based on your results during the experiment, or use a more rigorous extrapolation model that considers seasonality and other factors.

A simple method

Brandon Anderson from Adobe uses the following formula:

Incremental revenue per visitor × visitors per day × 365 days = incremental annual revenue

Let's look a little deeper into the two variable inputs (I've shortened "revenue per visitor" to RPV for convenience):

▶ Incremental RPV = Winner RPV − Control RPV

▶ Visitors per day = Total visitors in the experiment ÷ number of days the experiment ran

Here's a worked example:

▶ 300,000 visitors

▶ 14 days in the experiment

▶ Control RVP = $5.00

▶ Winner RVP = $5.50

Incremental revenue per visitor × visitors per day × 365 days = incremental annual revenue

($5.50 − $5.00) × (300,000 ÷ 14) × 365 = $3,910,714

Apply the "chop it in half" filter

With the above calculation, many assumptions are involved. For example, you know visitors won't be at a consistent level for the year, and while your experiment is controlled, not everything will remain the same beyond the experiment duration.

> Applying the "chop it in half" filter makes your results much more conservative.

Giving a conservative estimate is a good idea, because the only safe thing with any forecast is that it will be wrong:

▶ Original figure = $3.9 million

▶ 50 percent of original figure = $1.95 million

Incremental annual revenue with the chop in half filter applied = $1.95 million.

Great! Now you have a conservative figure to use as a guide to demonstrate the value of your experiment.

Recommendation

As we discussed in Chapter 1, experiments are worthwhile only if they have a clear outcome and you take responsibility for bringing that outcome to fruition. Key to making that action happen is a confident recommendation, alongside your clear results message, about what should come next.

Hopefully this is change you can influence immediately, and your recommendation will be as simple as one of the following:

Results and recommendation(s)

▶ **Significant benefit** Release the challenger.

▶ **Detrimental impact** Plan the next wave.

▶ **No difference** Prevent the challenger going live; plan the next wave.

Takeaway

▲ Use a clear headline to communicate the results.

▲ Monetize your results to demonstrate the value of your experiment.

▲ Give a strong recommendation to encourage the action required.

Expect challenges

Finding winners in your experiments inevitably draws challenges, particularly when results don't go as planned, or have an undesirable outcome. Let's look at challenges you can expect.

When stakeholders don't get the results they wanted

When experiments go the stakeholders' way, they will love experimenting; you're proving the value of their work and contributing to their success. It's not always as easy when experiments don't go their way; one thing you can rely on is that they'll challenge the data.

In Chapter 1, we discussed how you might choose to revisit experiments yourself to see how they hold up over time. No doubt, you'll also end up revisiting experiments simply because they have been challenged, and you need to provide extra evidence to give more confidence in the data.

When results have undesirable outcomes

You might hope that a significant winner in an experiment is all you need to make change happen and push the winner live. Unfortunately, you'll still face challenges sometimes. Even when you have empirical data showing the right thing to do, you'll meet resistance to a change that has undesirable outcomes for some.

As we've just discussed, it's crucial to make your results headline and recommendation clear, especially when your results are challenged. Unclear or overcomplicated results won't help you persuade stakeholders that this is the right decision.

A/A test

A good way to demonstrate confidence in your results is to run continual A/A tests (**Figure 8.1**). An A/A test is simply an experiment that has no change between the variants. That is, customers are randomly assigned to two instances of the same thing, and the difference is measured. Of course, you'll expect the difference to be close to zero, allowing for some random fluctuation.

A/A Experiment

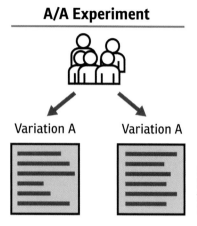

Variation A   Variation A

Figure 8.1 Continual A/A testing will help build confidence in your testing framework and thus instill confidence in your results.

A/A testing helps prove the robustness of your method and approach. By showing that changing nothing gets you no significant difference, you also show that changing something can be attributed as the reason for differences observed.

Takeaway

▲ Expect challenges when results don't go as planned or have undesirable outcomes.

▲ Continually run A/A tests to demonstrate confidence in your method and approach.

Unexpected results

The purpose of an experiment is to prove your hypothesis to be correct, but sometimes you'll find positives you didn't expect. Here we'll look at unexpected results.

When a feature makes no difference

There is no such thing as a "neutral" new feature or addition to your website. Adding something always comes at a cost. Adding things adds overhead, whether its adding complexity to the code base and making future development harder, distracting customers' attention for no return, or simply using real estate on your website that could be better used in a new experiment for something that will add value. In experiment results, no difference in performance from the control usually means it's worse. Implement only the winners.

Accidental positives

If you find a positive outcome that you didn't expect, or that didn't form part of your hypothesis, it's important to treat those results carefully.

Experimenting is great for uncovering unexpected learning, but react to that learning only with a new experiment and a new hypothesis about the unexpected result.

Don't share the unexpected positive in the results of the current experiment, or you risk reacting to noise (and introducing uncontrolled change) or not understanding exactly the change you're affecting on your website and why it is driving certain behavior.

Implementing negative experiments

Usually it's simple: don't implement a negative or flat experiment. But that gets trickier if the result is flat or even a little negative but stands in the way of something else.

> Why would [Amazon] switch to buttons that don't convert as well?
>
> Because conversion isn't the only metric that matters. If you look closely, you'll notice they made the "Ready to Buy" area take up about half the space of the previous version. Why? Because they quietly launched a marketplace to resell used goods, deciding it would boost profits if they didn't have to stock and ship everything themselves.
>
> *"Hidden Secrets of the Amazon Shopping Cart," Bryan Eisenberg, FutureNow*

Sometimes you'll be faced with a quandary: should you release a small negative (perhaps a smaller Add to Basket button) to enable other features or improvements that you feel will provide a benefit (for example, to make space for a Compare feature)? Perhaps the negative is small but the change has other benefits you can't measure in your experiment, like customer satisfaction. Maybe you're confident your experiment that was flat has a benefit creatively that your brand will benefit from.

Takeaway

▲ "No difference" means worse. Ship only winners.

▲ If you find an unexpected positive, experiment again.

▲ Sometimes you'll have to release small negatives.

Sharing results

Now you have some results and you'll want to talk about them. Let's consider some of the implications of sharing results.

Sharing around your business

As you introduce an experiments program at your business, sharing results and learning across all areas is crucial for getting buy-in, generating excitement about experiments, and shifting toward a culture of experimenting on everything.

Promote what you're doing and the results you're getting, both positive and negative, at every opportunity. Any noise or buzz you can make for experimenting will help keep it in focus, and focus is required to build a culture. Experiment programs that sit quietly in the background as a service are the ones that fail.

The benefits of sharing around your business are many. Experiment results can often be used beyond your work; they can feed into the offline world, or optimize business workflows and align focus. Most importantly, however, sharing and discussing experiments will encourage others in your business to share ideas that could be the start of your next win.

Sharing externally

Many people share their experiment results online or with others outside the business. Sharing is great for developing the industry, great for your peers, and great for getting some learning in return that may inspire your next experiment win.

But there's a downside. Sharing your experiment results is sharing the competitive advantage your experiment efforts give you.

> Your experiments are an asset with real value to your business. Think carefully before you make them available to your competitors.

The businesses with the most sophisticated experiment programs, like eBay, Amazon, Booking, Google, Zynga, Facebook, Etsy, and Netflix, keep experiment results and learnings close to the chest. In fact, in some of these businesses, results of experiments are so sacred and protected they are available only to selected people within the business.

Takeaway

▲ Share and promote experiments internally to increase engagement, build maturity, and encourage ideas.

▲ Be careful what you share outside your business; experiment results are one of your most valuable resources.

Reacting to results

The key to any experiment program is reacting to results quickly and with as little effort as possible. Consider every finished experiment as the building block for a new experiment.

The message for those of us who are not tactically deployed in a testing role is that a commitment to testing should be central to how you run your business. ...In reality, it takes a concerted, sustained effort; from picking the right things to test, to running clean testing, to having people who can digest the results and add their own insights. Once the commitment to a "testing culture" is made, getting consistent, repeatable methodology in place for the entire process—from conception to application of results—is key to the overall success of the business.

"A/B Testing: It's not about the results, and it's definitely not about the why,"
commenter Bill Wagner, Signal vs Noise, the 37signals blog

Let your results from the first experiment inform you, then move quickly to a new wave where you test other alternatives of your winning or losing challenger.

Reuse learning

Finding a winner is great, but even better is understanding the hypothesis that drove that winner and how you can reuse that learning in other areas of your website or business.

Keep a knowledge base of things you learn and discover in your experiments, and review it often to consider other places where these new learnings can be introduced to drive more value.

Reuse experiment code

All your experiments require at least some development and build. Can you repurpose that in the next wave or in another test? The iterative nature of experimenting lends itself well to reusing code and assets.

Keep an archive of experiment code and assets for reuse. Reusing code will speed up development of the next wave, and increase your capacity for experimenting. You'll also start to develop a pattern library of code and assets that provided winners, making reuse of those elements even more efficient and useful!

Takeaway

▲ Take advantage of the continuous and iterative nature of experiments.

▲ Start planning the next experiment wave immediately.

▲ Reuse code, assets, and learning to get the most of your experiment efforts.

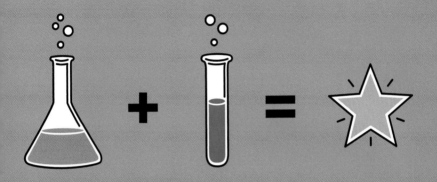

9

Conclusion

Getting started

Every day we conduct many little experiments that help us determine a winner and make decisions, like trying a new coffee, testing a new washing-up liquid, trying on some new clothes, or taking a different journey home to try to save some time. For businesses, making decisions through controlled experiments is a surefire way to make choices that have the desired impact on the bottom line.

It's easy to get started: start small, and start with the obvious. Focus first on elements that play a big role in conversion. Create challengers for them, and then devise tests to pit one challenger against one incumbent. Once you have a lineup, be sure to clearly state your goal and hypothesis so that you can know conclusively whether the challenger has succeeded or failed.

To be effective, experiment with elements or features of your website that the majority of users interact with, and expose enough visitors to the experiment to reach conclusive results. As you rapidly test and demonstrate measurable improvements in your site's low-hanging fruit issues, stakeholders will come to see the value of experimenting. Work to build a culture of experimenting, and be sure your recommendations are implemented so your business can get the benefits.

The complexity of your experiments will grow over time as you develop your skills in the craft. A/B testing, a straightforward comparison of one factor to one other equivalent factor, will deliver the rapid results you need when your testing program is just starting. Multivariate testing, which involves two or more independent factors, yields deeper insights and is a great addition as your experiment program matures. Once you've decided which of these two approaches to use for your experiment, the next step is simply to start the experiment and begin to gather the data. The amount of exposure your experiment gets will determine the length of time it will have to run to collect enough data for meaningful analysis. It's important not to end your experiments too soon because if your data sample isn't large enough, your results will be meaningless, and likely nothing more than random noise from natural fluctuations in your website's performance over a period of time. Fortunately, duration calculators make it easy to see how long you'll need to test to find meaningful results. They're provided by some of the vendor tools you'll be working with to analyze your data. I've given you an overview of those tools, from free to enterprise to home-brewed, in Chapter 3.

Interlude

When your site was designed, the user experience was integrated into it and considered holistically. The danger is that the small incremental changes suggested by testing will cause the UX to drift away from the design's original intent. You can guard against this by occasionally pulling back to look at the big picture. Be clear on what the big picture for your site is, and take opportunities to bring any wandering elements back into a unified whole. Remember, your big picture will have to be repainted often, as you learn through experiments what works and make generalizations to inform your design decisions.

Be unbiased in choosing design ideas to test, and be unbiased in interpreting the results. You can't be emotionally attached to a design you are trying to improve. Sometimes a design that's clearly better in your eyes isn't the winner. This can be hard to accept, but that standard of objectivity is also your friend when it's necessary to defend your site against design by committee or a senior stakeholder whose expertise is in another area. It's a lot easier to stand your ground for an experiment result with a quantifiable value than for a design decision that's difficult to make clear to nondesigners. It's also easier to decline to implement a stakeholder idea that was tested and turned out not to be the best choice.

Successful experiments require good ideas. Ideas can be stimulated by qualitative data such as usability reports and customer feedback or quantitative data such as analytics and data from your previous experiments. Design ideas can also be simply intuitions or serendipitous connections among things you've observed. Best practices, challenging assumptions, features your customers are used to from their social networks and devices, and the UX of the world around us can all generate ideas worth testing. Always be on the lookout for ideas wherever you are, and capture everything using your favorite note-taking method. Be sure to welcome collaborators with a wide range of approaches who are willing to focus with you on a common goal. Appreciate them for their contributions and for the buy-in their involvement encourages from a variety of stakeholders.

Moving forward

Data collection is the easy part, and you can now gather an almost unlimited amount of data about your site performance, interactions, and activities. To make sense of the data, it's necessary to separate out the signal from the noise and focus on the parts that are relevant to your inquiry. Luckily there are some methods to help you do just that. Statistical significance is an important measure of validity. You can also reinforce the validity of your data by measuring how much variance there is over several data-collection periods and whether it's steady, and by accounting for any atypical events that would have affected your data.

Segment your data to gain further insights. Your experiment data will become your most valuable data, and it will give you many ideas about what to test next. You may learn that a feature is popular with repeat visitors but virtually ignored by new visitors, or that copy has good results in one channel but not in others. Be sure to filter out traffic that isn't coming from actual customers, such as internal traffic and spiders. Finally, take timing into account to avoid looking at skewed data and drawing the wrong conclusions.

The last step is the most important one: turn your experiments into actionable recommendations and see experiment wins get implemented. Keep your message clear, and put a monetary value on your results so people take notice. Don't be concerned about presenting results that some stakeholders may find disappointing. Share your findings freely within your business to gain visibility, reputation, and commitment to experimenting for the long term, but remember, your results are valuable assets to your business; consider the implications of sharing them with your competitors.

We've covered a lot of ground. The promise of experimenting is in the confidence it gives you to optimize and innovate with measurable feedback that proves the value of your design decisions. Hopefully this overview gives you the confidence to begin or grow your experiment efforts. From here on, you could get the data quicker than you could have a meeting about it. Experiment!

10

Recommended
Reading

Publications and talks

Ron Kohavi

At Microsoft, Ron publishes some fantastic papers on experimenting, with practical advice on the lessons learned and pitfalls to watch out for. Required reading as you look to improve your approach and build a culture of experimentation.

http://robotics.stanford.edu/~ronnyk/ronnyk-talks.html

Always Be Testing: The Complete Guide to Google Website Optimizer

Bryan Eisenberg and John Quarto-vonTivadar

Bryan Eisenberg and John Quarto-vonTivadar's book on A/B testing is a great introduction to the subject. It's focused on Google Website Optimizer, but the practical advice they provide can be applied with any tool. With 250 testing ideas included, this is the book for you if you're looking for specifics of what exactly to test.

Do It Wrong Quickly: How the Web Changes the Old Marketing Rules

Mike Moran

Mike Moran shows you how to try lots of little things, analyze the results, learn quickly from your failures, and do it all over again. As failure is such an important part of experimenting, this will make a useful field guide and companion.

Don't Make Me Think: A Common Sense Approach to Web Usability

Steve Krug

Krug's instant classic on web usability serves as a good reminder about how to build a website that is easy to use. Take note as you build experiments to improve the user experience. You'll also find practical advice on running simple usability tests to find user problems you can address through experiments.

Scientific Advertising
Claude C. Hopkins

Claude C. Hopkins believed advertising should be measurable. In the first decade of the twentieth century, he pioneered experimentation with sales copy. His fundamental principles will give you endless ideas for experiments with copy and headlines.

Influence: The Psychology of Persuasion
Robert B. Cialdini

Cialdini explains the six psychological principles that drive an impulse to comply. The best book on the science of persuasion, this is essential reading as you look to build persuasion into your experiments to create a website that converts.

Neuro Web Design: What Makes Them Click?
Susan M. Weinschenk

Weinschenk applies the research on persuasion and decision making to the design of websites, and shows you how to actually implement these powerful ideas. This book is full of inspiration for experiments.

Predictably Irrational: The Hidden Forces That Shape Our Decisions
Dan Ariely

Dan Ariely takes you through some fascinating and surprising experiments from the field of behavioral economics that will make you rethink how you think, and question the common assumption that people behave in a rational way. You'll certainly begin to consider the profound effects of behavior in your experiments.

Nudge: Improving Decisions About Health, Wealth, and Happiness

Richard H. Thaler and Cass R. Sunstein

Thaler and Sunstein demonstrate that when people behave in irrational ways, some gentle nudging techniques can change their behavior. A straightforward primer on behavioral economics to help you consider the implications in your experiments.

How We Decide

Jonah Lehrer

Jonah Lehrer offers an accessible account of how we make decisions from decades of research in neuroscience and behavioral economics. Understanding how your customers make decisions, or how they choose, is an invaluable skill for designing successful experiments.

The Wisdom of Crowds: Why the Many Are Smarter Than the Few

James Surowiecki

James Surowiecki will show you how the aggregation of information in groups results in decisions that are often better than could have been made by any single member of the group. A must-read as you move decision making from the HiPPO to the crowd (your customers).

Analog In, Digital Out: Brendan Dawes on Interaction Design

Brendan Dawes

Brendan Dawes will take you through his creative process and how he comes up with ideas and designs for interactive experiences, usually with a lot of playing and experimenting. A must-read for anyone charged with coming up with ideas for a living.

The Myths of Innovation

Scott Berkun

Scott Berkun attempts to debunk the myths that surround innovation to give you a pragmatic guide that's really all about hard work and crafting your ideas. A great book for anyone brave enough to innovate, and a useful starting point as you begin to challenge and improve your website by experimenting with new ideas.

Web Analytics: An Hour a Day
Avinash Kaushik

Avinash Kaushik's fantastic guide to web analytics, showing you how to gain actionable insights from your analytics efforts, build a data-driven culture in your business, and feed your experimentation and testing program with data-driven ideas.

Google Analytics
Justin Cutroni

Justin Cutroni shows you how to get the most out of Google Analytics, whether you're new to it or have been using it for years. It will help you configure the system to measure the data most relevant to your business goals, helping you more accurately identify the best opportunities for experimenting.

How to Lie with Statistics
Darrell Huff

Darrell Huff's handy reference for anyone dealing with statistics serves as either a refresher or a quick introduction. As you present results, you'll appreciate this book's insights on the niceties of presenting graphs and charts in a persuasive way.

The Wall Street Journal Guide to Information Graphics: The Dos and Don'ts of Presenting Data, Facts, and Figures
Dona Wong

Dona Wong offers a step-by-step guide to creating clear and concise graphics to convey messages eloquently and effectively. This book will help you help your audience make sense of the numbers when you are presenting your results.

Acknowledgments

This book is largely the product of running thousands of experiments and taking hundreds of notes along the way. It's a privilege to see these ideas find a place in the Voices That Matter series.

I'd like to thank the team at Peachpit: Michael Nolan for believing I was the authority for a Voices That Matter book on A/B and multivariate testing, for allowing me to write the book I wanted to, and for assembling such a strong team at Peachpit for the project. Rose Weisburd for her dedication, her help in shaping these ideas, her advice and guidance, and her support throughout. Mimi Heft for taking care of the cover and interior design, for getting it right every time, and for her patience and understanding as I insisted on things like "make the gold star look more gold."

I'd also like to acknowledge those who've directly or indirectly helped shape this book: Shalini Kesar for her mentorship during my thesis as part of my degree. While other lecturers rejected the idea that an approach could exist for measuring and *valuing* the user experience and design choices we make, Shalini encouraged me to go with it. Our early discussions on approaches and methods paved the way for all that has followed and planted the seeds for this book. Brendan Dawes for showing me that "best practice" was there to be broken and that everything can be an experiment. What I learnt from Bren changed the way I think about design, and his book *Analogue In, Digital Out* made me want to write a book with New Riders. Ron Kohavi for his feedback while reviewing the draft manuscripts of this book and for his endorsement and support of the book you hold in your hand right now. Ronny has long been an inspiration. I continue to learn from his work and am proud to count him as a new friend. Thomas Høgenhaven and Andreas Høgenhaven for help with some illustrations used in the book. Also, thanks to the businesses I've worked with, for allowing me to experiment and hone my craft on their websites, with their customers, and with many colleagues who've taught me something about designing and creating successful websites.

Finally, thank you to my wife Elizabeth, for her support and encouragement in everything I do.

Index

WATCH
READ
CREATE

Unlimited online access to all Peachpit,
Adobe Press, Apple Training and New
Riders videos and books, as well as content
from other leading publishers including:
O'Reilly Media, Focal Press, Sams, Que,
Total Training, John Wiley & Sons, Course
Technology PTR, Class on Demand, VTC
and more.

No time commitment or contract
required! Sign up for one month or
a year. All for $19.99 a month

SIGN UP TODAY
peachpit.com/creativeedge